GOD'S WONDERFUL PEOPLE

More Christian Assemblies for Schools

Michael Forster

First published in 1996 by
KEVIN MAYHEW LTD
Buxhall
Stowmarket
Suffolk IP14 3DJ

© 1996 Kevin Mayhew Limited

The right of Michael Forster to be identified as the author
of this work has been asserted by him in accordance
with the Copyright, Designs and Patents Act 1988.

All rights reserved. No part of this publication may
be reproduced, stored in a retrieval system, or transmitted,
in any form or by any means, electronic, mechanical,
photocopying, recording or otherwise,
without the prior written permission of the publisher.

The drama sections of this book may be photocopied
without copyright infringement, provided they
are used for the purpose for which they are intended.
Reproduction of any of the contents of this book
for commercial purposes is subject to
the usual copyright restrictions.

ISBN 0 86209 757 6
Catalogue No 1500044

Editor Alison Sommazzi
Cover design by Jennifer Carter
Typesetting and Page Creation by Vicky Brown
Printed in Great Britain

Foreword

Following the success of *Wonderful World*, it seemed appropriate to produce this second volume. Most, although not all, of the stories are taken from *Good Night, God Bless* which was intended as a family bedtime book. In this version, the stories are presented as dramas as well as narratives, and suggestions are made for involving the class in the preparation of the assembly. It is assumed that one class will be leading assembly for a wider group of children, perhaps the whole school. If this is not the case, then minor adaptations will need to be made

As with the earlier books, all the bible stories have been imaginatively rewritten while retaining and emphasising the original meaning. I hope that this not only makes them more enjoyable as stories in themselves but also, in many cases, brings out other dimensions of the biblical texts. They are intended to be fun, but to make serious points. To this end the dialogue is deliberately modern and often colloquial in order to make the characters as recognisably like real people as possible, rather than dim figures from the distant past, speaking in conventional religious language. It is also intended to make the stories entertaining and hold the children's attention so that the essential points can be conveyed and remembered. It is of course open to individual readers to adapt the words to a style which best suits their own personalities or situations

I believe that material for use with children should be both accessible and satisfying for people of every age. So while I hope that these stories will communicate well with quite young children, they also have other layers of meaning which may speak to older children and adults as well.

Some of the stories are very freely adapted indeed, and a few have been transposed into the present day. Since they are not intended to be read consecutively, but separately in different assemblies, this should not cause confusion.

It has been a highly enjoyable task to produce this book; I hope it may be at least equally enjoyable to use, enabling pupils and teachers to enjoy working and worshipping together.

MICHAEL FORSTER

Sources

The songs recommended in these assemblies come from one of the following sources.

SS: The song section of this book

WUW: *Wake Up, World!* by Michael Forster and Christopher Tambling (Kevin Mayhew)

WW: The song section of *Wonderful World!* by Michael Forster (Kevin Mayhew)

A: *Alleluya!* by David Gadsby and John Hoggarth (A & C Black Ltd.)

CAP: *Come and Praise* Complete Edition by Geoffrey Marshall Taylor and Douglas Coombes (BBC Books)

The songs suggested are merely a sample of what is available in these and other publications, and the lists are far from exhaustive. They provide the busy teacher under pressure with a ready source of ideas for appropriate songs. However, if time permits a more thorough search, there is a wealth of further resources available.

Contents

		Page
Foreword		3
Sources		4

Old Testament

Let it Be	*Genesis 1*	8
Oh Brother!	*Geneses 4:1-12*	12
Rabbles and Babbles	*Genesis 11:1-9*	16
Don't Ask Me!	*Exodus 3:1-4:16*	20
You Can't get Water from a Stone	*Exodus 17:2-7*	24
A Little Yellow Idol	*Exodus 32:1-24*	28
The Donkey's Tale	*Numbers 22-24*	32
All I Want is a Baby	*1 Samuel 1:1-20*	36
Appearances Can Be Deceptive	*1 Samuel 16:1-13*	40
Whose Baby?	*1 Kings 3:16-28*	44
Elijah's Last Journeys	*2 Kings 2:1-15*	48
Room at the Top	*2 Kings 4:8-17*	52
Life's Like That!	*2 Kings 4:18-37*	56
Keep it Simple	*2 Kings 5:1-14*	60
Live Connections	*Ezekiel 37:1-14*	64

New Testament

Trials and Temptations	*Matthew 4:1-11*	68
Jesus Makes Matthew Rich	*Matthew 9:9-13*	72
Don't Be Stingy!	*Matthew 13:1-9*	76
The Barley and the Bindweed	*Matthew 13:24-30*	80
The Sale of the Century	*Matthew 13:45-46*	84
Jesus Gets Angry	*Matthew 21:12-14*	88
Nancy's Nightmare	*Matthew 25:31-end*	92
'Are You a Friend of Jesus?'	*Matthew 26:30-39, 51-58, 69-75*	96
The Voice in the Wilderness	*Mark 1:1-11*	100
Perfectly Willing to Learn	*Mark 7:24-30*	104
Speechless With Surprise	*Luke 1:5-25, 57-64*	108

The Women's Story	*Luke 1:26-40*	112
Questions! Questions!	*Luke 2:41-end*	116
Silly, Snobbish Simon	*Luke 7:36-end*	120
Poor Ebenezer!	*Luke 12:16-21*	124
Airs and Graces	*Luke 14:7-11*	128
Don't Be Taken In	*Luke 16:1-9*	132
Ben and Neb get Better	*Luke 17:11-19*	136
Keep Your Wig On, Judge!	*Luke 18:2-5*	140
Representation and Reality	*Luke 18:9-14*	144
Noncommittal Nick	*John 3:1-8*	148
Wait for the Power	*Acts 2:1-21*	152
A Disciple in the Desert	*Acts 8:26-39*	156
God Has No Favourites	*Acts 10*	160
The Angel, the Apostle and the Great Escape	*Acts 12:1-19*	164

Songs

Get With the Beat	171
Jesus Can Make Us Truly Rich	171
Let it Be!	172
Rabbles, Babbles	173
Questions! Questions!	173
Be Yourself!	174
God Doesn't Want	175
Dry Bones	176

Let it Be
Based on Genesis 1

BEFORE THE DAY

Get the children involved *together* in something creative. You could make up a large sheet of paper and get them to cooperate on a painting. Or is there an area of the school or grounds that they could brighten up? If so, take some photographs while they're doing it, to make a display for the assembly.

- Think about the actions for all the children to join in during the story.

ON THE DAY

Introduction

Today we're going to hear the story about how God created the world. We've been getting creative, too, but more of that later. First, we're going to say our 'Thank you' prayer.

'Thank you' Prayer

Thank you, God, for all you give us,
thank you for the earth and sea;
thank you, God, for special people,
thank you, God, for making me.

God's Story

Before God made the world, it was very, very dark. The universe was shapeless and had no life in it, except for God. In the silence, the only sound was of God breathing. Then God spoke.

'Let there be light!'

And suddenly, there was light everywhere. Just imagine having all the lights in your street burning in your bedroom. It was brilliant! The trouble was, there was no one there to see it, except God. But he was working on that.

God looked at the light, and said, 'That's pretty good, but it wouldn't do to have it always. I know. I'll create time.' So he divided up light from darkness. 'There,' he said. 'That's the day, and I'll call *that* the night.' So the evening came, and then the morning, and that completed the very first day. But things were still in a pretty disordered state – a bit like most children's bedrooms, only a million times worse! So God decided it was time to do some sorting out. 'There', he said, when he had finished, 'I'll call this part "heaven".' By that time it was evening, and after that came another morning: the second day had gone.

Well, there was an awful lot of water sloshing about in the world, and God decided that was the next bit to be tidied up. 'Let's get all the water together,' he said, 'and make a bit of dry land. I'll call the dry bits "earth" and the watery bits "sea". My Word, that looks good!' Then God really started to get going! 'Now, let's see what this earth can produce!' he said. 'Give me some plants!' And it happened. 'Give me some seeds,' said God. And it happened. 'Give me some fruit!' And before long, the earth was covered with wonderful green plants, and brightly coloured fruit: red strawberries, yellow bananas – what else can you think of? 'Well, bless me!' thought God. 'This is really good!' But by now – yes, you've guessed it – the evening had come again. Then came the morning, and that was the third day taken care of.

Well, the earth was looking pretty spectacular. So God looked around at the sky and thought, 'Perhaps I should spruce this up a bit. Let's have some stars, and planets around here. And they'd better move round in circles to mark the seasons – otherwise we'll end up with May blossom in November or something equally silly.' And d'you know, people still use them for that, all these centuries later. So God provided a bright light for the day, and a dimmer one at night – just enough to stop it being too frightening. By then it was evening again, and God said, 'Well upon my Word – that's a good day's work!' Then he waited for morning. The fourth day had gone.

Now there were all kinds of plants and flowers on the earth, wonderful stars in the sky, but the sea was looking a bit empty. So God spoke to the sea. 'Let's see what you can do,' he said. 'Give me lots of animals – great big sea monsters, and whales and sharks, and octopuses. And let's have some birds in the air as well.' And before you could say – well, you couldn't say anything because people hadn't happened yet – but anyway, there were fish and birds all over the place.

- The fish *swam*
- the eels *wriggled*
- and the birds *flapped their wings*

God said, 'That's right – make yourselves at home, and let's have lots of you – I want plenty of life in the world!' And then what do you think? That's right – it was evening again. and the fifth day was over.

When morning came, God looked at the earth, and said, 'Come on – let's have some life around here! Don't leave it all to the sea.' And that's exactly what happened. Every kind of wild animal – everything from dinosaurs to dingoes! And God was pleased – but not *that* pleased! 'What would really top it off,' he said, 'would be people. Human beings, made like me, able to love and be loved, who would be my special friends. They'd be able to help me – we could do things together. They would be the best of all the things I've made.' So God made men and women; he made them able to love, and able to think, and said, 'Come and be my special friends and helpers. Share my work of making this creation a wonderful place to be. Look, I've given you great things – plants and fruit and rocks, wonderful colours, and everything you could ever need. Look after it well, and work with me to make it even better.'

And so it was. God looked at everything he had made, and thought, 'Even though I say it myself, it's pretty terrific!' The sixth day had passed.

Then the morning came again: the seventh day. And what do you think God did then? He had a rest!

Our Story

Show the assembly what the class has done, and describe how it relates to the story: how they had to work together, arrange things in proper order, separate things out, etc.

Prayers

We're Sad

We're sorry, God,
for all the things that spoil your world.
Sometimes we forget just how beautiful
and how fragile it is.
Forgive us, and help us
to care for your creation.

We're Glad

The world's a wonderful place:
full of colour, and light and life.
Thank you for making it beautiful in so
many ways.
And thank you especially
for letting us help you.

Let's Pray for People

There are some people who can't see or hear
the beautiful things in the world.
And some just don't notice,
because they're too busy.
Please God, help all people
to enjoy your creation
in lots of different ways.

Songs

Let it be (SS)
God made the earth (WUW)
We can plough and dig the land (WUW)
God is making a wonderful world (WUW)
Morning has broken (CAP)
Think of a world without any flowers (CAP)
Somebody greater (CAP)

Let it Be

God's Story

Narrator	Before God made the world, it was very, very dark.
God	Let there be light!
Narrator	And suddenly, there was light everywhere.
God	That's pretty good, but it wouldn't do to have it always. There. That's the day, and I'll call *that* the night
Narrator	So the evening came, and then the morning, and that completed the very first day. But things were still pretty messy! So God did some sorting out.
God	There, I'll call this part 'heaven'.
Narrator	By that time it was evening, and after that came another morning: the second day had gone. But there was an awful lot of water sloshing about in the world.
God	Let's make a bit of dry land. I'll call the dry bits 'earth' and the watery bits 'sea'. My Word, that's good! Now, let's see what this earth can produce! Give me some plants! Give me some seeds! Give me some fruit!
Narrator	Before long, the earth was covered with wonderful green plants and brightly coloured fruit: red strawberries, yellow bananas – all sorts of things.
God	Well, bless me! This is really good!
Narrator	The evening had come again. Then came the morning, and that was the third day taken care of. The earth was looking pretty spectacular. So God looked around at the sky.
God	I'll spruce this up a bit. Let's have some stars, and planets around here. And they'd better move round in circles to mark the seasons – otherwise we'll end up with May blossom in November or something equally silly. We'll have bright light for the day, and a dimmer one at night. Well upon my Word – that's a good day's work!

Narrator	Now the fourth day had gone. The earth looked great, but the sea was looking a bit empty.
God	Let's see what the sea can do. Give me lots of animals – great big sea monsters, and whales and sharks, and octopuses. And let's have some birds in the air as well.
Narrator	Straight away, there were fish and birds everywhere. • The fish *swam* • the eels *wriggled* • and the birds *flapped their wings*
God	That's right – make yourselves at home, and let's have lots of you – I want plenty of life in the world!
Narrator	Now the fifth day was over. When morning came, God looked at the earth again.
God	Come on – let's have some life around here! Don't leave it all to the sea.
Narrator	And so there were animals – everything from dinosaurs to dingoes! And God was pleased – but not *that* pleased!
God	What would really top it off would be people. Human beings, made to be like me, able to love and be loved, to be my special friends. We could do things together. They would be the best of all the things I've made.
Narrator	So God made men and women; he made them able to love, and able to think.
God	Come and be my special friends. Look, I've given you great things – plants and fruit and rocks, wonderful colours, and everything you could ever need. Look after it well, and work with me to make it even better.
Narrator	The sixth day had passed and God was pleased with everything he had made.
God	Even though I say it myself, it's pretty terrific! A good week's work by any standards. Bless me! Is that the time? I think I'll have a day off.

Oh Brother!

Based on Genesis 4:1-12

BEFORE THE DAY

Think about ways of belonging and caring. Are any of the children cubs or brownies, or perhaps in the Boys' or Girls' Brigade? Get them to collect badges, logos etc. from any appropriate organisations they can think of, and make a display. Don't limit them unnecessarily. Greenpeace or WWF, for example, give a creation-wide dimension to this.

• Think about the actions for all the children to join in during the story.

ON THE DAY

Introduction

Today we're going to think about belonging, caring and taking responsibility. First, we're going to say our 'Thank you' prayer.

'Thank you' Prayer

Thank you, God, for all you give us,
thank you for the earth and sea;
thank you, God, for special people,
thank you, God, for making me.

God's Story

Adam and Eve had two sons. The first one's name was Cain, and when he was born Eve was really proud. Then about a year later they had another baby, and called him Abel. The two boys were very much like ordinary children, really. They sometimes played together, and at other times they would argue and fight. Most children grow out of this kind of silliness, but still, Eve was anxious.

'I worry about those two,' she said. 'One of these days one of them's going to get badly hurt in their arguments.'

'Oh don't exaggerate!' Adam replied. 'You worry too much. It's just the way children are. We were young once, you know.'

'No we weren't,' said Eve. 'That's the problem with being the first people God made.'

'There you are, then!' retorted Adam. 'What d'you know about children? Leave them alone.'

That wasn't very helpful of Adam, was it? Well, Cain and Abel grew up from children into young men and they were still quarrelling and getting jealous of each other. Eve got really worried. 'They'll never survive if they carry on like this,' she said. Then Adam had an idea.

'I know. We'll teach Abel to be a shepherd and Cain to be a gardener,' he said. 'Then they won't be able to get jealous of one another because they'll be doing such different things.'

- Cain learned to *scatter seeds*
- and to *clip hedges*
- Abel learned to *shear sheep*

Eve thought that was a wonderful idea, and decided that everything was going to be all right after all. She didn't realise how wrong she was!

The boys grew into men, and still they didn't learn not to fight all the time. Eventually, Eve's worst fears came true.

When Abel's sheep had their first lambs, he said, 'I must give some of them to God, as a way of saying thank you.'

Well of course Cain immediately decided that he should give some of his crops as well. If Abel was going to give God a wonderful present, then Cain would make jolly sure he gave God a better one! So Cain went and got the best crops he had grown. 'I'll make God like me more than he likes Abel,' he thought slyly.

So the day for the offering came and Abel brought some beautiful young lambs and offered them to God. Just as he was doing it, he heard a voice behind him say, 'Come on, God – get a load of this, then!' Abel turned round and there was Cain staggering along pushing a great big barrow loaded with all the fruit and vegetables you can imagine *(such as . . .)*

Cain staggered up to where Abel was, dropped the handles of the barrow and gasped, 'There! Better than a few silly little lambs, eh!'

God did not like this one little bit. 'Abel just wanted to give me a present,' he said, 'but you did it because you were jealous of him. So it's Abel's gift that pleases me most.'

Now I've seen some spoilt children in my time, but when it came to throwing tantrums Cain could have been a gold medallist! He jumped up and down; he waved his arms in the air; he threw himself on the ground and hammered the earth with his fists. After a little while, God said, 'Why are you so angry?'

'Why am I so angry?' Cain spluttered. 'I bring you barrowloads of food, and Abel brings a few scruffy little lambs, and you prefer his present to mine – and then you ask why I'm angry!'

'Look,' said God, 'if you're going to get like this every time you lose then you're going to end up in real trouble. I'd watch that temper if I were you.'

Cain didn't like that, but he hadn't got an answer so he just bottled it all up and plotted to get his own back on Abel. One day he suggested a nice walk in the country. Abel thought that must mean they were friends again, so he said, 'That's a good idea,' and off they went.

As soon as they got out of sight of the house, Cain pretended to have cramp in his foot and got behind Abel. He picked up a big sharp stone and he attacked Abel from behind, bringing the stone down on his head as hard as he could. Poor old Abel didn't stand a chance; he went down and lay very still. Cain knew that he was dead.

It's strange how things that seemed like a good idea at first often don't look so good afterwards. What was Cain to do? He couldn't bring Abel back to life, and he really wished he hadn't got so carried away. But there was nothing to be done, now.

As Cain was going back towards his house, he heard God speaking to him: 'Cain, where's your brother?'

Cain made what he thought was a very clever reply. 'Who am I,' he asked, 'his keeper?'

'That's a silly question,' said God. 'Abel's never needed a keeper, but he's often wanted a brother.'

'I'm his brother,' replied Cain.

'Exactly,' said God. 'Now where's Abel?'

Cain was really frightened now. 'Um – er – I – ah,' he gabbled.

'Don't try to fool me,' said God. 'You've killed him. I warned you to watch that temper of yours. You know what you've done, don't you? You can't face your parents now, so you're going to have to go and live somewhere else. And for the rest of your life you'll be a guilty person, on the run.'

So that's how it turned out. How Cain wished he'd listened to God and learnt to control his temper!

Our Story

Show the children the display, and get them to identify some of the logos and say how those particular organisations fit into today's theme. Could joining one of these be a way of taking on a little more responsibility?

Prayers

We're Sad

Please, God, forgive us
when we feel jealous of other people's success.
Help us to be glad for them,
to share their happiness,
and to learn from them.

We're Glad

Thank you, God,
for making us all brothers and sisters
to one another.
Thank you for all the joy we get
from sharing our lives.

Let's Pray for People

All over the world,
people are finding things to fight about.
Please God, bless the people
who are trying to find answers
and to bring peace.

Songs

God said, 'Cain, where is your brother?' (WUW)
Thank you, O God, for all our friends (WW)
Where have all the flowers gone? (A)
Magic penny (A)
Make me a channel of your peace (A)
When I needed a neighbour (CAP)
The family of man (CAP)

Oh Brother!
God's Story

Narrator	Adam and Eve had two sons, called Cain and Abel. Sometimes the boys played together, and at other times they would argue and fight, and they often used to get jealous of one another.
Eve	I worry about those two. One of these days one of them's going to get badly hurt in their arguments.
Adam	Oh don't exaggerate! You worry too much. It's just the way children are. We were young once, you know.
Eve	No we weren't! That's the problem with being the first people God made.
Adam	There you are, then! What d'you know about children? Leave them alone.
Narrator	That wasn't very helpful of Adam, was it? Well, Cain and Abel grew up from children into young men and they were still quarrelling and getting jealous of each other.
Eve	They'll never survive if they carry on like this.
Adam	I know. We'll teach them separate trades, so they can't compete.
Narrator	So that's what they did.

- Cain learned to *scatter seeds*
- and to *clip hedges*
- Abel learned to *shear sheep*

Narrator	Even when they grew up into men, the boys wouldn't stop fighting. The real trouble happened when Abel's sheep had their first lambs.

Abel	I'll give some of the lambs to God, to say thank you.
Narrator	Straight away, Cain had a bad thought.
Cain	I'll make God like me more than he likes Abel.
Narrator	Abel brought some beautiful young lambs and offered them to God. Then he heard a mean voice behind him.
Cain	Come on, God – get a load of this, then! I've brought you some wheat, some bread, carrots, potatoes, apples, pears – better than a few silly little lambs, eh!
Narrator	God did not like this one little bit.
God	Abel just wanted to give me a present, but you did it to get one up on him. So I like Abel's gift best.
Cain	*(Aside)* I'll get Abel for this! Just see if I don't. *(To Abel)* How about a nice walk in the country?
Narrator	As soon as they got out of sight of the house, Cain picked up a big sharp stone, and killed Abel with it. Then he turned to go home.
God	Cain, where's your brother?
Cain	Who am I – his keeper?
God	That's a silly question. Abel's never needed a keeper. But he's often wanted a brother.
Cain	I'm his brother.
God	Exactly. Now where's Abel? You've killed him, haven't you? Well, you can't face your parents now, so you're going to have to go and live somewhere else. And for the rest of your life you'll be a guilty person, on the run.
Narrator	So that's how it turned out. How Cain wished he'd learnt to control his temper!

Rabbles and Babbles

Based on Genesis 11:1-9

BEFORE THE DAY

Think with the children about great human achievements: obvious ones with child-appeal like computers and space travel, but other ones as well: transplant surgery and penicillin (children once used to die from what are now much less serious illnesses); social reforms (how would the children like to have to clean chimneys by climbing up them?) Perhaps the children themselves could research one of these subjects and draw some pictures. You could also teach the children to say a simple phrase in various languages, and then let them shout them out together where indicated.

• Think about the actions for all the children to join in during the story.

ON THE DAY

Introduction

Soon, we're going to hear about some people who tried to be too clever, but first we're going to say our 'Thank you' prayer.

'Thank you' Prayer

Thank you, God, for all you give us,
thank you for the earth and sea;
thank you, God, for special people,
thank you, God, for making me.

God's Story

A long, long time ago, in a land called Shinar, some people had what they thought was a great idea. They believed that all they had to do was work together, and they could do anything. And since everybody spoke the same language, working together should have been easy. 'Why,' said Barnaby, 'with our combined knowledge and skills, we could climb right up to heaven!'

Barnaby's friend, Johnny, wasn't so sure. 'To begin with,' he said, 'how do you know exactly where heaven is?'

'Oh, don't be stupid!' said Barnaby, crossly. 'Heaven's got to be up there; it's not down here, so that's the only place left.'

'I know it looks that easy,' said Johnny, 'but things might not be quite as they seem.'

Barnaby was impatient. 'Look,' he said, 'it's very simple. What you see is what there is. Don't make things complicated by asking unnecessary questions. This is earth, and heaven's up there. That's how it looks, and that's how it is.'

Johnny didn't like arguing with Barnaby, but he couldn't resist saying, 'Perhaps God doesn't want us to climb up to heaven – if that's where it is. Perhaps that's why we can't see it.'

Barnaby thought this was the silliest idea he'd heard so far. 'Of course God wants us to do it!' he said, scornfully. 'Would he have made us so wonderfully clever, and taught us how to build towers and things if he didn't want us to do it?'

Johnny opened his mouth to speak, but Barnaby held up his hand. 'No more!' he said. 'We have a duty to use all the knowledge we have. That's what God expects. So whatever we're capable of doing must be right.'

Johnny thought, 'I'm capable of punching you on the nose, but it wouldn't be right to do it!' But he didn't say that, because he knew Barnaby would have an answer. Barnaby always did!

So everyone set to work – everyone except Johnny and Barnaby, that is.

- The designers *drew the plans*
- the stone masons *hammered and chiselled*
- the carpenters *sawed the wood*

God wasn't happy about it, though. He hadn't put people on earth so that they could spend all their time trying to get back to heaven! He could see what was really happening, and he didn't like it. The people who were building the tower were so obsessed with it that they forgot about everything else. They never played with their children, or looked after their elderly relations. They started to think that the tower was all that mattered. Some people even died from neglect. All the workers were interested in doing was trying to get to heaven! So God got very angry. 'I'm going to teach them a lesson,' he thought.

So it was that, one morning, Barnaby got up and went out as usual to find a very unwelcome surprise awaiting him. He'd have known about it earlier if he'd listened to his wife that morning, but he never did that. As he got near to the tower, he heard the most amazing sound – a loud babbling of lots of people all shouting at one another at the tops of their voices. So Barnaby went up and tried to silence them, but he had to get a whistle and blow it before they noticed him. When they did, he started telling them off.

'You're supposed to be building this tower,' he shouted at them, 'not gossiping amongst yourselves – now get on with it!'

Barnaby couldn't understand why the people were looking at him in such a strange, bewildered way. Then the foreman came up and spoke to him, and it was Barnaby's turn to look amazed. He couldn't understand anything the foreman was saying. 'What's the matter with you?' he yelled at the foreman. 'Talk properly so that I can understand you.'

The foreman couldn't make out what Barnaby was saying, and realised that Barnaby couldn't understand him either. So he tried again – but louder. Barnaby still couldn't understand and he shouted back – louder still. Then all the others joined in, and before long everyone was shouting at everyone else, and nobody was listening.

You know what had happened, don't you? They were all speaking different languages! Everything everybody said made sense – but only to them! No one could understand anybody else at all![1]

So the tower never got finished.

And it won't be. God is still trying to teach us that heaven isn't in the sky; the way to find heaven is to care about other people, and learn to understand each other.

And all this time later, we're still not very good at it!

[1] If prepared, the children shout their phrases here.

Our Story

God's got nothing against skills – it's what we do with them that's important. Show and tell the whole assembly what the class has learnt.

Prayers

We're Sad

Sometimes we think we're more important than anyone else in the world.
Then it ends up with us all shouting at each other and nobody listening to anyone else.
We're sorry, God.
Please teach us to be good listeners.

We're Glad

Loving God,
everyone matters to you.
We don't need to work at it.
You don't mind if we're not clever.
You just love us, as we are.
Thank you, God.

Let's Pray for People

We pray for people who get forgotten,
people who are in trouble but don't get noticed;
people whose voices get lost
in all the noise others are making.
Please God, help us to hear them,
so that we can show them
how important they really are.

Songs

Rabbles, babbles (SS)
I'm black, I'm white, I'm short, I'm tall (WUW)
Thank you, O God, for all our friends (WW)
Let there be peace on earth (A)

Rabbles and Babbles
God's Story

Narrator	A long, long time ago, everyone in the world spoke the same language – until Barnaby had his bright idea.
Barnaby	You know, Johnny, if we all worked together we could do anything – even climb right up to heaven!
Johnny	That's ridiculous. How do you know heaven's up there? It might be more complicated than you think.
Barnaby	Oh, don't be stupid! Heaven's got to be up there; it's not down here, so that's the only place left. And where d'you think all that light comes from?
Johnny	I know – but things aren't always as they seem.
Barnaby	You're a philosopher.
Johnny	That's a rotten thing to say!
Barnaby	Look, it's very simple. This is earth, and heaven's up there. That's how it looks, and that's how it is.
Narrator	Johnny didn't like arguing with Barnaby, because he always felt so inferior; Barnaby seemed to know so much, and to be so confident, and Johnny always ended up feeling silly. Still, he tried again.
Johnny	Perhaps God doesn't want us to climb up to heaven. Perhaps that's why we can't see it.
Barnaby	Don't be stupid – if God didn't want us to do it we wouldn't be able to.
Johnny	(*Aside to audience*) I'm *able* to punch him on the nose, but that doesn't mean God would want me to do it!
Narrator	So *nearly* everyone set to work. Johnny didn't join in because he thought it was wrong, and Barnaby thought *he* was too important.

Barnaby	I'm an ideas man. I must save my creative energy, and let less important people do the actual work.
Narrator	Surprisingly, most of the other people joined in. They were very impressed by Barnaby's confidence, and thought Johnny was a very silly man.

- So the designers *drew the plans*
- the stone masons *hammered and chiselled*
- the carpenters *sawed the wood*

Narrator	God knew what was happening, and he didn't like it.
God	I didn't put people on earth so that they could spend all their time trying to get back to heaven! These people are obsessed! They never play with their children, or look after their elderly relations. I'll teach them a lesson and give them something else to think about.
Narrator	So it was that, one morning, Barnaby got up and went out as usual to find an unwelcome surprise awaiting him. He'd have known about it earlier if he'd listened to his wife, but he never did that – he just used to get up and rush straight out to see how the tower was getting on. As he got near to the tower, he heard a loud babbling – lots of people all shouting and yelling at one another.
Barnaby	You're supposed to be building this tower, not gossiping amongst yourselves – now get on with it!
Narrator	Soon, they were all shouting at one another and getting nowhere because they were all speaking different languages! No-one could understand anybody else at all! Just imagine it[2].
Barnaby	Now the tower will never get finished.
Narrator	God is still trying to teach us that heaven isn't in the sky; the way to find heaven is to care about other people, and learn to understand each other. And all this time later, we're still not very good at it!

[2] If prepared, the children shout their phrases here.

Don't Ask Me!

Based on Exodus 3:1-4:16

BEFORE THE DAY

Let the children imagine being asked to do something they didn't want to do (*that* will not be difficult!) What excuses might they use to avoid it? Write them down in large letters on the left hand side of a flip chart. Now let them imagine that they want to do something, but have to persuade you to let them. What might they say, then? Write those arguments down in the right hand column. Make it a game, and enjoy a good laugh with them, thus encouraging them to think of more outlandish answers. Note when they run out and start to repeat themselves!

• Think about the actions for all the children to join in during the story.

ON THE DAY

Introduction

You wouldn't make excuses if you didn't want to do something, would you? We're going to see some very interesting examples in a few minutes, but first we'll say our 'Thank you' prayer.

'Thank you' Prayer

Thank you, God, for all you give us,
thank you for the earth and sea;
thank you, God, for special people,
thank you, God, for making me.

God's Story

Moses was having a nice quiet life. The rest of the Hebrew people were terribly unhappy, because they were slaves in Egypt, but Moses had escaped from that and he was working as a shepherd. Apart from chasing the odd wolf away, life didn't get very exciting; he just walked from place to place finding grass for the sheep to eat. Mind you, that was hard work, but Moses never complained because most of the time it was safe, even if it was a little boring.

One day, he was out minding the sheep when he noticed something strange. A bush nearby seemed to be on fire, except that it wasn't going all black and shrivelled the way bushes normally do when they burn. So he thought he'd take a closer look. Then he had the shock of his life – he heard a voice.

'Hey! Moses!'

'What!' exclaimed Moses, looking all round. 'Where did that come from?'

'I'm over here!' said the voice.

Surely, it couldn't be the bush talking, could it? It was really scary! Moses was about to run away when the voice came again.

'Come over here, Moses. I want to talk to you. But take your shoes off, first, because this is holy ground.'

Holy ground! Of course! It was God who was speaking. Mind you, it might have been better if it had been the bush; when God gives people visions he usually has a job for them! Moses did as he was told; he took off his shoes and went closer.

'That's better,' said God. 'Now we can talk properly. I've been watching what's been going on in Egypt.'

'Lucky you,' thought Moses. 'I haven't seen a good cabaret dancer in years.' But that wasn't what God was talking about. God was very unhappy about the way the Hebrew slaves were being treated, and had decided to set them free. Moses got worried.

'I hope you're not going to ask me to get involved in politics,' he said, 'because I don't think it mixes with religion.'

'Oh, not that cop-out again!' sighed God. 'If you had any idea how often I've heard that! Look, people are suffering, and I want to do something about it. And you're going to help me.' This was getting a bit heavy, and Moses really felt he would prefer to talk to the bush, but it wasn't to be. Then he heard the words he'd been dreading.

'You're to go and see Pharaoh,' said God, 'and tell him to let the people go.'

'Go and see who? And tell him what?' squeaked Moses, who was very frightened by now. 'I can't do that! It's all right for you, but I have to live in this world! Anyway, you need a good orator – an experienced politician. I just know what'll happen when I get in front of the king: I'll get all tongue tied – that's if he doesn't cut it out first.'

God wasn't going to listen to that kind of talk. 'Come on, Moses,' he said, 'trust me. I'll be right with you the whole time.'

Things weren't going Moses' way. So he decided to try another approach.

- He *scratched his head*
- and then he *shook it from side to side*
- Suddenly he *snapped his fingers.* Got it!

He put on his most reasonable and worldly-wise voice – the way people do when they know they are wrong. 'Well of course, God, the reality is,' he said, 'that these people have never heard of you. They've been in slavery all their lives, and I'm afraid we need to face up to the situation as it really is – they've forgotten you. I mean, what am I going to say if they ask who you are? Have you got a name?'

God wasn't falling for that. 'Oh no you don't, Moses!' he said. 'You can't put a label on me, like a plant or an animal. I'm greater than any name you could think of. *I* decide who and what I am, and I will be whoever I choose – you go to the slaves and tell them that! And say that I'm going to set them free!'

Moses was getting desperate by now, and he started to repeat himself: 'But no one's going to listen to me!' he wailed. 'I'm a terrible speaker – you ask my wife about that, she'll tell you! No one will take notice of me. Look, I've got a nice home, a lovely wife, and a good, steady job. That's the kind of bloke I am. I'm not into . . .'

'If you mention politics again, you'll regret it!' said God, and the bush seemed to burn more fiercely than before. 'I care about people – and if you're a friend of mine you will, as well. Stop trying to wheedle out of it and do as I ask.' Then the voice got gentler again. 'Look, Moses, I know you're frightened, but I wouldn't ask you to do it if I wasn't going to back you up. If it makes you feel better, you can take Aaron with you – he can talk.'

'That's true!' said Moses. 'He could talk the humps off a camel, could Aaron.'

'That's settled then,' said God. 'Now go and find Aaron, and let's get cracking. We're going to set the people free!'

And that is exactly what they did. But that's a much longer story.

Our Story

Show the children the flip chart, and tell them about the fun you had making it. You can see Moses going through the same process in the story, and eventually starting to repeat himself. You might speculate as to how he would have tried to persuade God, if the boot had been on the other foot.

Prayers

We're Sad

We're sorry God.
Sometimes we say, 'I can't'
when we mean 'I won't'.
When people are in trouble,
we make excuses for not helping them.
Show us what we can do,
and help us to trust you.
Oh, and don't take 'No' for an answer!

We're Glad

Thank you, God, for not giving up,
even when we do.
Thank you for helping us
to be good friends to one another.

Let's Pray for People

We know that some people are unhappy,
perhaps because other people are cruel to them,
or because they are poor, or ill.
Please show us what we can do to help,
and then give us the faith to do it.

Songs

God said, 'Folks, we're going walkabout' (WUW)
Lead my people to freedom! (WUW)
We're all going to the Promised Land (WW)
Moses, I know you're the man (A)
Give me oil in my lamp (CAP)
The journey of life (CAP)
One more step (CAP)

Don't Ask Me!
God's Story

Narrator	Moses was having a nice quiet life. The rest of the Hebrew people were terribly unhappy, because they were slaves in Egypt, but Moses had escaped from that and he was working as a shepherd. One day, he was out minding the sheep when he noticed something strange. A bush nearby seemed to be on fire, except that it wasn't going all black and shrivelled the way bushes normally do when they burn. So he took a closer look. Then he had the shock of his life – he heard a voice.
God	Hey! Moses! Over here.
Moses	What's that? Surely, not the bush talking!
God	Come over here, Moses. I want to talk to you. But take your shoes off, first, because this is holy ground.
Narrator	Holy ground! Of course! It was God who was speaking. Mind you, it might have been better if it had been the bush; when God gives people visions he usually has a job for them to do! Moses did as he was told; he took off his shoes and went closer.
God	That's better. Now we can talk properly. I've been watching what's been going on in Egypt.
Moses	*(Aside)* Lucky him! I haven't seen a cabaret in years.
God	Not that! I'm going to set the slaves free – and you're going to help me.
Moses	I hope you're not going to ask me to get involved in politics, because I don't think it mixes with religion.
God	Oh, not that cop-out again! If you had any idea how often I've heard that! Look, people are suffering, and I care! Go and see Pharaoh and tell him to let them go.
Moses	Go and see who? And tell him what? I can't do that! It's all right for you, but I have to live in this world!

	Anyway, you need a good orator – an experienced politician. I just know what'll happen when I get in front of the king: I'll get all tongue tied – that's if he doesn't cut it out first.
God	Trust me, Moses. I'll be right with you the whole time.
Narrator	Things weren't going Moses' way. So he tried to think of another approach. • He *scratched his head* • And then he *shook his head* • Suddenly he *snapped his fingers.* Got it! Moses put on his most reasonable and worldly-wise voice – the way people do when they know they are wrong.
Moses	Well of course, God, the reality is that these people have never heard of you. They've been in slavery all their lives, and I'm afraid we need to face up to the situation as it really is – they've forgotten you. I mean, what am I going to say if they ask who you are? Have you got a name?'
God	Oh no you don't, Moses! You can't put a label on me, like a plant or an animal. I'm greater than any name you could think of. *I* decide who and what I am, and I will be whoever I choose – go and tell the slaves that!
Moses	But no one's going to listen to me! I'm a terrible speaker – you ask my wife about that, she'll tell you! No-one will take notice of me. Look, I've got a nice home, a lovely wife, and a good, steady job. That's the kind of bloke I am. I'm not into . . .
God	If you mention politics again, you'll regret it! I care about people – and if you're a friend of mine you will, as well. Take Aaron with you – he can talk.
Moses	That's true! He could talk the humps off a camel, could Aaron.
God	That's settled then. Now go and find Aaron, and let's get cracking. We're going to set the people free!

You Can't get Water from a Stone

Based on Exodus 17:2-7

BEFORE THE DAY

Let the children have fun drawing some cartoons which show people complaining in opposite circumstances: in the heat and in the cold, in drought and in flood, becalmed sailors and someone with an umbrella in a gale, and so on. What examples can they think of themselves? Perhaps some could make up stories about 'Mr. Never-Satisfied'!

- Think about the actions for all the children to join in during the story.

ON THE DAY

Introduction

Soon, we're going to hear about some people who were always complaining; but first, we'll say our 'Thank you' prayer.

'Thank you' Prayer

Thank you, God, for all you give us,
thank you for the earth and sea;
thank you, God, for special people,
thank you, God, for making me.

God's Story

You remember Moses, don't you? He was the man whom God used to lead the Israelites out of Egypt. The trouble was that the people thought he was going to solve all their problems in one go. They'd been slaves all their lives and they thought that Moses was going to make everything wonderful. Just like that. They didn't realise that that isn't the way God usually works.

Whatever happened, the people were never satisfied. If there was no breeze, they complained about the heat, and if there was one they whined about sand being blown in their faces. During the day, they moaned about the weight of their luggage; and then at night they complained that they hadn't got enough blankets to keep warm!

One day, Moses said to God, 'I'm fed up with this. Why couldn't you have left me alone? I enjoyed being a shepherd.'

'Oh, come on, Moses,' said God. 'Don't start all that again. I took you from being the leader of a few sheep and made you the leader of a nation.'

'I'd have preferred the sheep,' said Moses. 'On the whole they're probably more intelligent than this lot. And they never moaned at me.'

'If you want to be a great leader, you've got to cope with that,' God answered.

'But I *don't* want to be a great leader,' said Moses, in despair. 'I was happy as a shepherd, minding the sheep and my own business.'

'Were you?' asked God. 'You knew that your brother and sister, and all your people were slaves and were being ill treated – and you wanted to do something about it. You just didn't think you were capable of it.'

'And I'm not!' said Moses.

'I know you're not,' said God, 'but I am. And all you need to do is trust me. Anyway, stop arguing because you've got visitors.'

Moses looked round and, sure enough, an angry looking crowd were approaching, and leading them was the chief agitator.

'Oh, no!' said Moses. 'It's that Simon character. He's been making trouble ever since we left Egypt.'

'Hey, Moses! shouted Simon. 'We want a word with you. We're thirsty.'

'Well, stop shouting, then,' said Moses, 'or you'll make it worse.'

Simon didn't like that at all. 'Don't you get clever with me,' he snarled at Moses. 'We're all fed up with your high and mighty ways.'

'Look,' said Moses, 'I told you we'd get to the Promised Land, and we will.'

'When?' asked Simon, aggressively.

'I don't know,' Moses answered.

'This year? Next year? Sometime? Never?' taunted Simon. 'All right, then – where is it?'

'What d'you mean?' asked Moses.

'Good grief!' said Simon. 'He doesn't even understand plain Hebrew. Watch my lips, Water-baby! WHERE IS THE PROMISED LAND?'

'How should I know?' said Moses.

'You're the one who's leading us there,' yelled Simon. 'Of course you should know!'

'Don't be idiotic, Simon,' said Moses. 'D'you think I put that pillar of cloud and fire in the sky? God's the one who's leading us, and he knows where we're going.'

'Look,' said Simon, 'if you've got God on your side, what about a bit of water – that's not much to ask, is it?'

Then all the others started to join in.

(Have a few children primed to lead the barracking.)

- Simon: What do we want?
- Children: *Water!*
- Simon: When do we want it?
- Children: *Now!*
  (Repeat ad lib)

'Okay, God,' said Moses. 'You told me to trust you. Now what do I do?'

'Simple,' said God. 'Get some water out of one or those rocks.'

Moses wondered whether the heat had got to God, as well! 'What!' he answered. 'Get water out of a stone? That's impossible.'

'Look, Moses,' said God, 'I could get blood out of a stone if I wanted to, but water will do for now. Stop arguing and do as I say. Hit one of those rocks with your stick.'

Moses was really angry, and he would rather have hit Simon, but instead he raised his stick and brought it down as hard as he could on the rock.

'Temper, temper!' scolded Simon.

He had hardy got the words out when he heard a strange gurgling sound and a trickle of water came out from the rock. Just as Simon and his friends ran forward excitedly, all fighting to get the first drink, there was a great, thunderous crash and the stone face split wide open as a rush of water came pouring out. Simon was knocked right off his feet, and ended up rolling around in a big puddle of muddy water. Everyone else thought it was really funny, and whenever Simon tried to stand up someone pushed him down again. He had wet sand in his clothes, in his shoes, in his hair, in his ears and in his mouth. And it tasted horrible!

'There you are, Simon,' laughed Moses. 'All the water you could want. That'll teach you not to complain.'

But it didn't.

Simon and his friends found lots more to complain about – but I'll have to tell you about that another time.

Our Story

Show the assembly the cartoons, and/or let the children tell their stories. How often are we like 'Mr Never-Satisfied'?

Prayers

We're Sad

Please forgive us, God,
for being so silly!
When we've got water we waste it,
then we complain about the shortage.
And after that, we moan about the rain!
Please help us to be sensible, and grateful.

We're Glad

God, you're full of surprises!
Just when we think we know everything,
you show us something new.
Thank you for this wonderful world,
and the exciting things that happen in it!

Let's Pray for People

It's a funny thing, water.
Sometimes we love it, sometimes we hate it!
But we always need it.
In some places people die of thirst,
and some people get ill drinking dirty water.
Help us to learn to help one another.

Songs

Sing a song of weather (WW)
Wade in the water (A)
Raindrops keep fallin' on my head (A)
Water of life (CAP)
Desert rain (CAP)

You Can't get Water from a Stone
God's Story

Narrator	Remember Moses? He was the man who helped God set the Israelites free. The trouble was that the people thought he was going to solve all their problems in one go. And when he didn't, they all moaned at Moses.
Moses	I'm fed up with this, God. I never wanted the job in the first place – I told you I wasn't up to it.
God	I know you're not, but I am – so trust me. Anyway, you've got visitors and they don't look very happy.
Moses	Oh, no! It's that Simon character. He's been making trouble ever since we left Egypt.
Simon	Hey, Moses! We want a word with you. We're thirsty.
Moses	Well, stop shouting, then, or you'll make it worse.
Simon	Don't you get clever – we've had enough of that.
Moses	Look, I said we'd find the Promised Land, and we will.
Simon	When?
Moses	I don't know.
Simon	All right, then – where is it?'
Moses	Don't ask me – how should I know?
Simon	Well you're the one who's leading us there!
Moses	Don't be idiotic, Simon. God's the one who's leading us, and as long as he knows where we're going that's all that matters.
Simon	You're mad, you are. Just because you hear strange voices, you think God's talking to you. All right, then – if you've got God on your side, what about a bit of water? That's not much to ask, is it?'

Narrator	Then all the others started to join in.

(Have a few children primed to lead the barracking.)

- Simon: What do we want?
- Children: *Water!*
- Simon: When do we want it?
- Children: *Now!*

(Repeat ad lib)

Moses	Okay, God, you told me to trust you. Now what?
God	Simple – get some water out of one or those rocks.
Moses	What! Get water out of a stone? That's impossible.
God	Look, Moses, I could get blood out of a stone if I wanted to, but water will do for now. Stop arguing and do as I say. Hit one of those rocks with your stick.
Narrator	Moses was certainly ready to hit something! He raised his stick and brought it down hard on the rock.
Simon	Temper, temper! That won't get you anywhere.
Narrator	A tiny crack appeared in the rock, and a trickle of water came out. Everyone ran forward, fighting to get the first drink in case there wasn't enough to go round. Just as they got to the rock, there was a great, thunderous crash and it split wide open as a rush of water came pouring out. Simon was closest, and ended up rolling around in a big puddle of muddy water. Every time he tried to stand up someone pushed him down again. He had wet sand in his clothes, in his shoes, in his hair, in his ears and in his mouth. And it tasted horrible!
Moses	There you are, Simon – all the water you could want. That'll teach you not to complain.
Narrator	But it didn't.

A Little Yellow Idol

Based on Exodus 32:1-24

BEFORE THE DAY

Get the children to make models from scrap materials: computers from cardboard boxes, space rockets from kitchen roll cores, etc.

• Think about the actions for all the children to join in during the story, and if using the drama version rehearse the class to lead the assembly in the response.

ON THE DAY

Introduction

We're going to hear about some model makers who got a bit carried away. First, though, we're going to say our 'Thank you' prayer.

'Thank you' Prayer

Thank you, God, for all you give us,
thank you for the earth and sea;
thank you, God, for special people,
thank you, God, for making me.

God's Story

Moses was up a mountain, praying, and he had been there a very long time. He and God had a lot to talk about; the people weren't at all happy about being in the desert. They used to moan and grumble at Moses all the time, as though all the trouble were his fault. 'It's all very well,' Moses said to God, 'but I'm not really leading them, am I? You are. And yet they moan at me.'

'That's the way it is,' said God. 'They can't see me – and if they could they'd be too frightened to say anything – so they have a go at whoever they think is closest to me. Anyway, you'd better get to work. I've got a few rules to help you all live properly, and I want you to write them down on stone.'

'That's hard work, 'said Moses, 'Can't I use clay or something?'

'Stone,' said God, sternly. 'This has got to last.'

Meanwhile, down at the bottom of the mountain, Simon was stirring up trouble. But then, Simon always did. He'd always secretly thought that he would be a much better leader than Moses, so he kept on saying how useless Moses was. And at this particular moment, he'd got a crowd round him and was having the time of this life!

'We were better off as slaves!' he shouted. 'At least then we had our bed, board and guaranteed employment.'

'Yeah!' shouted everyone, forgetting that it wasn't actually *paid* employment!

'Moses is a fool!' Simon cried.

'Yeah!' responded all the people.

'Couldn't find his way along a straight line if it was signposted!' roared Simon.

'Yeah!' the people shouted, and then went all quiet and embarrassed because of course they should have shouted 'No'!

'How much longer are we going to go on following him?' asked Simon. Then he turned to Aaron. 'Well, you're Moses' brother, aren't you – what are you going to do about it?'

Aaron was getting very frightened; he could see the crowd were really worked up. So he thought to himself, 'It wouldn't do any harm – just to calm things down until Moses gets back.' Then out loud, he said, 'All right – collect all the people's earrings, bangles, bracelets, anything at all that's made of gold. While that's happening, I'll make a mould.'

Up at the mountain top, God said to Moses, 'I think you'd better get back down there. Things are getting out of hand.'

'Oh, Aaron will handle it,' said Moses, who didn't really want to go back down yet.

'That's what you think!' said God. 'Go on, before I help you on your way. And don't forget to take the commandments with you.'

So Moses went back down the mountain, and when he got near the bottom he couldn't believe his eyes! All the people were singing and dancing and having a real party.

• Some were *banging the drums*
• Some were *blowing their trumpets*
• And some were *waving their arms about*

In the middle of it all was this strange looking statue which seemed to be a golden calf. Then, to his horror, he saw people bowing down to it and praying to it as though it were a god. He hurried down to where they were, and saw Aaron – his own brother – leading it all. Moses was really angry!

'Hey! Aaron!' he shouted. 'What's that thing?'

Aaron was frightened. 'Oh – well – er – it was the funniest thing,' he babbled. 'You'll laugh when I tell you.'

Moses didn't laugh.

'Well we just put our gold on the fire,' said Aaron, 'and out came this calf.'

Now you know and I know that it wasn't like that – Aaron gave it a lot of help!

'I'm not swallowing that,' said Moses. 'But you are.'

Moses strode to the altar, picked up the idol and started grinding it down. No one moved. They were wondering what Moses was going to do.

When the calf was just a heap of gold dust, Moses sent for some water, and poured out a cup for everyone present. Then he sprinkled the gold dust on the water.

'There you are,' he said. 'Drink it!'

The people were horrified. 'He doesn't mean it!' they said.

'Oh yes I do,' said Moses. 'If that thing was a god then it must be full of life and goodness. Now you can find out.'

And Moses made them drink every drop! They found out that it wasn't good at all.

Simon didn't say anything for a very long time after that. That was partly because he was so ashamed.

But it was mainly because his throat was sore.

Our Story

Show the children the models, and ask them to identify them. Then see if they work. Can the computer be switched on? Can the rocket rise under its own power? They're all very good models, no doubt, but they won't work like the real thing. Now what about the model of God? Oh, of course, there isn't one! We can't even begin to make that!

Prayers

Let's Chat

Having fun is important,
but do toys, video games or television
take up too much of our lives?

We're Glad

Thank you, God,
for the good things we have,
and especially for our family and our friends.
Help us to enjoy everything you give to us,
and always to put you and people first.

Let's Pray for People

Some people are unhappy
because they haven't got enough.
Other people are unhappy
because they worship money, or possessions.
Please God, teach us all to love each other
and to share the things that are really important.

Songs

God made the earth (WUW)
Out to the great wide world we go! (WUW)
Love is his word (A)
It's me, O Lord (A)
Somebody greater (CAP)
All things bright and beautiful (CAP)

A Little Yellow Idol
God's Story

Narrator	Moses was up a mountain, praying.
Moses	It's not fair, God. *You're* the boss, but *I* get moaned at.
God	That's the way it is. They can't see me, so they have a go at my friends. Anyway, you'd better get to work. I've got a few rules to help you all live properly, and I want you to write them down on stone.
Moses	That's hard work. Can't I use clay or something?
God	(*Sternly*) Stone. This has got to last.
Narrator	Meanwhile, down at the bottom of the mountain, Simon was stirring up trouble. But then, Simon always did. And at this particular moment, he'd got a crowd round him and was having the time of this life!
Simon	We were better off as slaves!
Children	Yeah!
Simon	Moses is a fool!
Children	Yeah!
Simon	Couldn't find his way along a straight line if it was signposted!
Children	Yeah!
Narrator	That got Simon confused, because he wasn't sure whether they should really have shouted 'no'!
Simon	Well, Aaron – you're Moses' brother, aren't you – what are you going to do about it?
Aaron	All right – collect all the people's earrings, bangles, bracelets, anything at all that's made of gold. While that's happening, I want two volunteers to help me make a mould. You and you will do.

Narrator	Up the mountain, God had finished talking to Moses.
God	I think you'd better go. Things are getting out of hand.
Narrator	When Moses got down the mountain, he couldn't believe his eyes! There was a big party going on, round a golden statue of a calf.

- Some people were *banging their drums*
- some were *blowing their trumpets*
- and some were *waving their arms about*

Narrator	Moses didn't mind that – or the dancing and singing. It was the statue he objected to.
Moses	Hey! Aaron! What's that thing?
Aaron	Oh – well – er – it was the funniest thing. You'll laugh when I tell you. We just put our gold on the fire, and out came this calf.
Moses	I'm not swallowing that – but you are.
Aaron	Eh?
Moses	Grind it down into dust, mix it with water and drink it.
Aaron	You don't mean it!
Moses	Oh yes I do. If that thing was a god then it must be full of life and goodness. Now you can find out.
Narrator	And Moses made them drink every drop! They found out that it wasn't good at all.
Moses	Right! You can think about that while I'm gone. I've got some more praying to do.
Narrator	And with that, Moses set off back up the mountain. Simon didn't say anything for a very long time. That was partly because he was so ashamed, but it was mainly because his throat was sore.

The Donkey's Tale

Based on Numbers 22-24

BEFORE THE DAY

Ask the children what they would like if they could wish for anything they wanted. Write up their wishes on a board, encouraging them to be as outrageous as they like, but be careful not to encourage false hopes!

- Think about the actions for all the children to join in during the story.

ON THE DAY

Introduction

In a few moments, we'll hear from a donkey whose owner wasn't very clever. First, we're going to say our 'Thank you' prayer.

'Thank you' Prayer

Thank you, God, for all you give us,
thank you for the earth and sea;
thank you, God, for special people,
thank you, God, for making me.

God's Story

I'm going to tell you a story, but you mustn't let on that it was me that told you. Why? Because we donkeys aren't supposed to know what's going on. It's a great life, being a donkey. Humans always think that they're the only ones who understand anything. So they talk about things in front of us and think it doesn't matter. Let me give you a tip: if you've got any secrets, don't talk about them in front of donkeys, because we've got long ears.

Anyway, I used to work for a man called Balaam. Yes, I know it's a funny name, but most people knew better than to laugh at it because it was said that Balaam could put a curse on you if he wanted to. Once he put curse on his next door neighbour – all over a misunderstanding. His neighbour used to call him Bally, and one day when he was talking about him somebody asked, 'Bally Who?' and everyone laughed. Balaam thought they were laughing at him and put a curse on his neighbour so that all his hair fell out. So now you know. Don't laugh at people with silly names. In any case, names like Amy and Jack would have sounded pretty strange in those days . . .

Now where was I? Oh yes – about Balaam. Well, I was standing in my usual place outside the window one day when I saw some visitors coming. I knew who they were straight away. I can tell the king's servants a mile off – all posh clothes and no brains. They told Balaam that the king was frightened because the Israelite army were on the way and looked as though they were going to invade. He wanted Balaam to put a curse on the army because he thought it would stop them.

Balaam sent them away with a flea in their ear. 'I don't believe God wants me to do that,' he said. But they'd hardly disappeared over the horizon when some more arrived. I could tell they were even higher officials than the last lot – posher clothes and even less brains. They were really having a go at Balaam. 'Can't you just come along and say what the king wants?' they asked. 'You don't have to mean it, just keep the old so-and-so happy so that we can get a bit of peace.' Well, Balaam kept on saying no, but eventually they got to him and – for the sake of peace and quiet – he decided to go with them.

Now I could have told him that this wasn't a good idea, but he wouldn't have listened. You see, humans have small ears and big mouths – that's their problem. Now if you look at a donkey, you'll find that our ears are bigger than our mouths which is the right way round. We listen a lot, but we say very little. And I knew we were heading for trouble.

Sure enough, we hadn't got very far when we hit a road block. And I don't mean any old road block. None of your silly poles across the road; this was an angel – ten feet tall, shining like a hoarding in Piccadilly Circus. So of course I did the sensible thing – I turned off into a field. Balaam went mad at me.

- He *jerked on the reins*
- He used his *whip*
- He *waved his fists in the air*

They it got worse: he kicked me, he shouted at me – and the language! Of course, I knew what the trouble was – Balaam's eyes are even smaller than his ears, and he couldn't see a ten-foot, digitally illuminated angel when it was right in front of him. I thought about telling him to open his silly eyes, but humans get so jealous of animals talking that I decided to keep mum. It didn't help, though, because we soon had the angel in front of us again, and this time there was nowhere to turn off. I tried to get through between the angel and the wall, but Balaam's foot got scraped against the stones and he yelled like mad. That's humans for you. They can drive nails into our feet, to fix shoes on, but if we so much as step on theirs they yell and shout fit to bust! By the next time I saw the angel, I'd had enough and I sat down. Balaam went mad! He started hitting me and kicking me, and I decided that was it. Like it or not, he was going to hear me talk.

'Are you potty?' I asked him. 'All these years I've been a good donkey to you – d'you think I'd do this for no reason?'

Of course, he looked more carefully then – and he saw it too. The angel wasn't very happy. 'What d'you mean by being cruel to a poor dumb animal?' he said. I wasn't sure that I liked the 'dumb' bit, but it's not often you get an angel on your side so I didn't complain. The angel went on, 'If it hadn't been for that donkey of yours you'd be dead by now.' Balaam was full of apologies, of course, and promised never to ill-treat me again. I'll believe that when I see it! Then he tried to turn me round and go home, but the angel stopped him.

'Carry on with your journey,' said the angel, 'but just be careful only to tell the king the truth – even if he doesn't like it.'

From what I gather, things got a bit silly after that, with Balaam refusing to say what the king wanted to hear, and the king trying to persuade him to do it. Eventually, the king realised it wasn't going to work and told Balaam to go home. Balaam was furious. 'All this way,' he said, 'and then he refused to listen to me just because I didn't say what he wanted me to. What do you think of that?'

Who? Me? Oh no! I know which side my bread's buttered. I kept quiet. And kept walking.

Our Story

Show the children the list of wishes and forecasts. Have any of the wishes come true? Almost certainly none of them will have, and the point can be made that merely wishing doesn't make things happen. How would the children have felt if they'd been promised those things and then let down? It's more important to be honest than to tell people what they want to hear.

Prayers

We're Sad

Loving God, please forgive us.
It's not always easy to be honest.
Then again, sometimes we're honest
in the wrong way, and we hurt people.
Help us to tell the truth,
and to be kind as well.

We're Glad

Thank you, God,
for people who are truthful to us
even when it's difficult.
It's good to have friends who care
enough to be honest with us.

Let's Pray for People

We pray for people
who have difficult jobs to do:
people who have to give advice
or to take decisions
which others might not like.
Please God, help them to be honest,
to do and say what they know to be right.

Songs

Out to the great wide world we go! (WUW)
Love is his word (A)
Nowhere man (A)
The best gift (CAP)

The Donkey's Tale
God's Story

Donkey   I'm going to tell you a story, but you mustn't let on that I told you because we donkeys aren't supposed to know things. It's great, being a donkey. Humans talk in front of us and think it doesn't matter. If you've got any secrets, don't mention them in front of donkeys, because we've got long ears.

               Anyway, I used to work for a man called Balaam. I was standing outside the window one day when I saw some important visitors coming. I can tell the king's servants a mile off – all posh clothes and no brains.

1st Servant   The king needs your help, Balaam. The Israelite army look as though they're going to invade.

2nd Servant   You've got to put a curse on them and stop them.

Balaam   I don't believe God wants me to do that. Go away.

Donkey   Then some more arrived: even higher officials than the last lot – posher clothes and even less intelligence.

3rd Servant   Can't you just come and say what the king wants?

4th Servant   Just to keep the old so-and-so happy.

Donkey   Well, eventually – for the sake of peace and quiet – he decided to go with them. Now I could have told him that this was a bad idea, but he wouldn't have listened. Humans have small ears and big mouths, whereas donkeys' ears are bigger than our mouths which is the right way round. I knew we were heading for trouble, and sure enough, we hadn't got very far when we hit a road block. And I don't mean any old road block. None of your silly poles across the road; this was a shining, ten foot angel. Of course, I did the sensible thing – I turned off into a field. Balaam went mad!

- He *jerked on the reins*
- He *used his whip*
- He *waved his fists in the air*

Balaam You stupid donkey! Get back on the road!

Donkey Now, Balaam's eyes are even smaller than his ears, and he couldn't see a ten-foot, digitally illuminated angel when it was right in front of him. I thought about telling him to look, but humans get jealous of animals talking. Then when I moved, so did the angel, and Balaam's foot got scraped against the wall.

Balaam Ow! That hurt! You stupid animal!

Donkey That's humans for you. They can drive nails into our feet, to fix shoes on, but if we so much as step on theirs they yell and shout fit to bust! Next time I saw the angel, I sat down. Balaam started hitting me and kicking me. Like it or not, he was going to hear me talk. 'Are you potty?' I said. 'All these years I've been a good donkey to you – d'you think I'd do this for no reason?' Then he got it from the angel as well.

Angel What do you mean by hurting a poor dumb animal?

Donkey Hey! who are you calling dumb?

Angel But for your donkey, you'd be dead by now.

Balaam I'm really sorry – honestly. I won't do it again.

Donkey I'll believe that when I see it!

Angel Carry on with your journey, but just be careful only to tell the king the truth – even if he doesn't like it.

Donkey Things got a bit silly after that. The king refused to listen, and Balaam moaned all the way home.

Balaam All this way, and he refused to listen to me just because I didn't say what he wanted. What do you think of that?

Donkey Who? Me? Oh no. I know which side my bread's buttered. I kept quiet. And kept walking.

All I Want is a Baby

Based on 1 Samuel 1:1-20

BEFORE THE DAY

Some of the children must have baby brothers or sisters. What kinds of things do the parents have to do to care for them? Get the children to bring to school examples of baby care items (perhaps empty packets) to form a display.

• Think about the actions for all the children to join in during the story.

ON THE DAY

Introduction

We're going to hear the story of Hannah in a few minutes, but first we'll say our 'Thank you' prayer.

'Thank you' Prayer

Thank you, God, for all you give us,
thank you for the earth and sea;
thank you, God, for special people,
thank you, God, for making me.

God's Story

Once there lived a man called Elkanah, who had two wives. One of them was called Hannah, and the other was called Pennina, which is a very nice name but she wasn't a very nice person. She had lots of children, and in those days people thought that that made you very special. Hannah had no children, and that meant that everyone looked down on her. Hannah was very unhappy, because she really longed to have a child of her own.

What made things worse was that Pennina kept on sneering at Hannah.

- She used to *point at her*
- and *stick out her tongue*
- and *make nasty faces*

'You've got no children,' she would say. 'You're useless – can't even do a simple thing like that.'

Elkanah didn't help, either. Whenever the big festivals came round, he always gave lots more presents to Pennina than to Hannah. Of course, he would never admit that he loved Pennina more than Hannah. He would try to explain by saying, 'She needs more than you do, with all those children of hers.' And that just made Hannah feel even worse! What a silly thing to say!

One day, when Hannah was really upset and was crying, Elkanah tried to comfort her, but he wasn't very good at that kind of thing and whenever he opened his mouth he put his foot in it. 'Why are you crying?' he said. 'I know you've got no children, but that doesn't matter. After all, who needs children when you've got me!'

That hadn't come out quite the way Elkanah meant it to, but Hannah didn't seem to notice. She was just angry. 'What d'you think's so special about you?' she said, through her tears. 'Just like a man to think you're all a woman could ever need!' Then she got up and ran out of the house. Elkanah started to run after her, but he was a bit out of condition and soon gave up.

Hannah ran to the place of worship. She was really upset and needed somewhere quiet to think. After she had been there a little while, she started praying. She didn't pray out loud, but just whispered the words so that no one else could hear. 'God,' she said, 'I really want to have a baby – I've always wanted one. If you let me have a child, I promise I'll nurse him well, and then as soon as he can eat ordinary food I'll give him to you. I won't mind – honestly – I'll be happy knowing I've got a child, even if I can't see him and play with him. I just want to be a mother. I promise I'll be a good one, for as long as he's with me. Then I'll give him to you and he can serve you for the rest of his life.'

You may wonder why she assumed that the baby would be a boy. Well, that's just the way people thought and spoke in those days. It was a man's world even before he'd been born! Come to that, a lot of people still think that kind of way now!

Anyway, back to Hannah. What she didn't know was that Levi, a priest, was standing watching her. He could see her lips moving, but no words were coming out. 'Oh dear!' he thought. 'Another drunk. They think they can come in here to shelter from the rain, and they always end up embarrassing me.' So he went over to Hannah. 'I think you'd better leave,' he said.

Hannah didn't know he was talking to her, and just kept on praying.

'Did you hear what I said? Out!'

Hannah still carried on praying, until she felt her shoulder being shaken. 'Come on,' said the priest. 'I said out! It really is too much: you drunks come in here, getting in the way, annoying the paying – I mean praying public.'

'Oh no, sir,' said Hannah. 'I'm not drunk, just terribly unhappy.' And with that, she burst into tears.

Underneath all his priestly dignity, Eli actually had a fairly soft heart. He put his arm around Hannah and tried to comfort her. 'I'm sorry,' he said, 'but we have to be careful here, you know. Do you want to talk about it?'

Hannah told him the whole story. Eli was very angry and began to raise his voice. 'Someone ought to give that Pennina woman a good talking to!' he said. 'And where's your husband – I'll give him a lesson in sensitivity!'

'Oh, no, please don't do that,' said Hannah. 'They're not bad people, really – and I do have to live with them afterwards, you know. Don't worry – I've said my prayer, and now I'll have to leave it to God.'

Eli smiled. 'Well, you may be right,' he said. 'Off you go home, and try not to worry. I've been working for God for quite a long time, and he hasn't let me down yet.'

After that, Hannah seemed happier. Pennina couldn't annoy her with her snide remarks about children any more, so she changed her tactics.

'You're putting on weight,' she said one day. 'Elkanah won't like that. And it's not as if you've got any excuse, is it? I mean, I've still got my figure even after having *all those children*.'

Hannah just smiled mysteriously. She had a pretty good idea why she was putting on weight, and she was very happy about it.

Sure enough, a few months later Hannah had her baby. It was a beautiful little boy, and she called him Samuel. Elkanah was over the moon. He was so proud of Hannah he could hardly stand still. 'My son,' he said. 'He's going to be a really great man – perhaps a farmer, or a camel driver.'

'No, he's not,' said Hannah. 'I promised him to God. And just as soon as he can feed for himself I'm going to take him to the priest.'

And Hannah kept her word.

Our Story

Draw attention to the display and show that wishing for a baby isn't like wishing for a new bike – babies bring a lot more responsibility with them!

Prayers

We're Sad

Sometimes we're cruel to people who are
    unhappy,
when we should be trying to help them.
Please forgive us, God;
help us to be kind to people,
even when we don't really understand.

We're Glad

Thank you, God, for people like Hannah,
who really love children.
And thank you for people like Eli
who know how to listen to people,
and who give us all faith.

Let's Pray for People

We pray for people who are sad,
because they can't have children
or because children have died.
Please, God, help us all
to love one another,
and to keep faith and hope alive.

Songs

God is making a wonderful world (WUW)
Out to the great wide world we go! (WUW)
Thank you, O God, for all our friends (WW)
Magic penny (A)
Hey, now, everybody sing! (A)
Sing hosanna! (A)
Morning has broken (CAP)
The best gift (CAP)

All I Want is a Baby
God's Story

Narrator Once there lived a man called Elkanah, who had two wives. Men were allowed to do that, in those days; but no one had heard of women's liberation, so women could only have one husband – and often they had to share him. One of Elkanah's wives was called Hannah, and the other was called Pennina, which is a very nice name but she wasn't a very nice person. She was very cruel to Hannah.

- She used to *point at her*
- and *stick out her tongue*
- and *make nasty faces*

Pennina You've got no children. You're useless – can't even do a simple thing like that.

Narrator Elkanah didn't help, either. He always gave lots more presents to Pennina than to Hannah.

Elkanah It's not that I love her more than you. She needs more than you do, with all those children of hers.

Narrator Now wasn't that a clever thing to say! Whenever Elkanah opened his mouth he put his foot in it.

Elkanah Why do you want children, when you've got me?

Narrator That hadn't come out quite the way Elkanah meant it to, but Hannah was too angry to notice.

Hannah Just like a man, to think you're all a woman needs!

Narrator She got up and ran out of the house to the place of worship. She was really upset and needed somewhere quiet to think and pray. She didn't pray out loud, but just whispered the words.

Hannah Please, God, if you let me have a child, I promise I'll nurse him well, and then as soon as he can eat ordinary food I'll give him to you.

Narrator	Hannah didn't notice Eli, an old priest, watching her.
Eli	*(Aside)* Oh dear! Another drunk. They think they can come in here to shelter from the rain, and they always end up embarrassing me. *(To Hannah)* I think you'd better leave. You're getting in the way, annoying the paying – I mean praying public.
Hannah	Oh no, sir, I'm not drunk, just terribly unhappy.
Narrator	With that, Hannah burst into tears. Underneath all his priestly dignity, Eli actually had a fairly soft heart. He put his arm around Hannah and tried to comfort her.
Eli	I'm sorry. Do you want to talk about it?
Narrator	Hannah told him the whole story. Eli was very angry.
Eli	Someone ought to give that Pennina woman a good talking to!
Hannah	Oh, no, please don't do that. She's not a bad person, really – and I do have to live with her afterwards, you know. Don't worry – I've said my prayer, and now I'll have to leave it to God.
Eli	Well, you may be right. Off you go home, and try not to worry. I've been working for God for quite a long time, and he hasn't let me down yet.
Narrator	Pennina carried on being nasty to Hannah.
Pennina	You're putting on weight. Elkanah won't like that. And it's not as if you've got any excuse, is it? I've still got my figure even after having *all those children*.
Narrator	Hannah just smiled mysteriously. A few months later she had her baby. It was a beautiful little boy, and she called him Samuel. Elkanah was over the moon.
Elkanah	He's going to be a really great camel driver.
Hannah	No, he's not. I promised him to God, and as soon as he can feed for himself, I'm going to take him to the priest.
Narrator	And Hannah kept her word.

Appearances Can Be Deceptive

Based on 1 Samuel 16:1-13

BEFORE THE DAY

How about a spot of nature study? Have the children ever seen a hoverfly, which looks like a wasp but can't sting? Or what about some toadstools that look like mushrooms but are definitely not good to eat? Do the children know of any examples? Perhaps they could use their imaginations to create a few (along the lines of the police box that became a time machine, for instance!) Get them to draw pictures of real or imaginary examples.

• Think about the actions for all the children to join in during the story.

ON THE DAY

Introduction

Things are not always the way they look. We'll be thinking about that in a few minutes, but first we're going to say our 'Thank you' prayer.

'Thank you' Prayer

Thank you, God, for all you give us,
thank you for the earth and sea;
thank you, God, for special people,
thank you, God, for making me.

God's Story

God had a dangerous job for Samuel.

'I've had it with king Saul,' God said. 'I want you to anoint a new king.'

'What!' said Samuel. I might be religious, but I'm not potty.'

'Oh, do stop going on, Samuel,' said God. 'I'm not asking for your opinion. I make the decisions round here, remember?'

'Sorry, God,' said Samuel, 'I suppose you're right as usual.'

'I'm right, as *always*,' said God, indignantly.

'Yes, of course, God. Sorry God,' said Samuel in an embarrassed sort of voice. 'How do you want me to do it, then?'

'Go and see old Jesse, the sheep farmer at Bethlehem,' answered God.

'Since when did anything remotely important happen in Bethlehem?' said Samuel.

'My Word!' God answered. 'You ain't seen nothin' yet!'

'Pardon?' asked Samuel.

'Never mind,' replied God. 'That's my favourite quotation, but it's after your time.'

Samuel mopped his forehead with his sleeve. 'Can we just get back to this Bethlehem thing?' he asked.

'Just do as I say,' said God. 'I'll tell you which one of Jesse's sons you're to anoint as king.'

Well,' said Samuel, dolefully, 'I really hope you know what you're doing, because if Saul finds out what we've done one of us is going to get killed. And since you're immortal, I've got a pretty good idea who it will be.'

So Samuel went to Bethlehem.

'Hello, hello, hello,' called Jesse. 'It's good old Sam the prophet man! What message of doom is it this time?'

'I'm just the messenger,' Samuel sighed, 'so if you want to moan, moan at God.'

'Silly bloke – can't take a joke!' said Jesse, and Samuel cringed. Jesse fancied himself as a poet – why, no one could understand. Samuel had heard that he'd got a talented son, but the gift clearly didn't come from his father.

'Look everything's all right. Okay?' he assured Jesse. 'Now send for your family.'

Jesse answered, 'All right, Sammy, keep your wig on; how'd I know there's something big on?'

'Oh dear,' Samuel thought, 'I'd better get on and do it, or Jesse will put me through it. Good grief! He's got me at it, now.'

Jesse's sons got ready to meet Samuel.

• They *washed their faces*
• and they *cleaned their teeth*
• and they *combed their hair*

The first son, Eliab, looked every inch a king. Tall and strong, and with clear, sparkling eyes, he fitted the part perfectly.

'Don't go by what you see,' God said. 'Appearances can be deceptive. I don't look at people the way you do. I look at the heart.'

'Oh, I should think his heart's fine,' thought Samuel. 'Healthy looking chap like that.'

'Don't get clever with me,' said God.

Before Samuel could think of anything else to think, Abinadab arrived and Jesse introduced him. 'This is my son – another one.'

'I've got to get out of here,' thought Samuel, reaching for his oil.

'Not so fast, sonny!' said God. 'Not him.'

So Jesse brought the next son over. 'This one is Shammah – takes after his mamma.'

Altogether, Jesse presented seven sons to Samuel, but God didn't choose any of them.

'Have you got any more?' Samuel asked Jesse, knowing he'd probably wish he hadn't.

'Yes,' said Jesse. 'Yes, there's another – he's their baby brother.'

'Well, you'd better get him,' sighed Samuel, 'but let *him* tell me his name.'

'Well, I don't know what you want with him,' said Jesse. 'He's not like the rest – you've looked at the best. I let him earn his keep by caring for the sheep.'

The youngest son came when he was sent for. 'Hello, he said, 'I'm David. I've heard all about you from my father.'

David was still quite young, and looked it. His hair probably hadn't seen a comb for days, and he seemed to be trying rather unsuccessfully to grow a beard.

'A nice lad,' thought Samuel, 'but . . .'

'That's the one!' God whispered, excitedly.

'I thought you said you knew what you were doing,' thought Samuel.

'No,' God corrected him. 'You said you hoped I did. I do, though – he's the one. Well, don't just sit there, get the oil out and do it. Then I'll let you get away from Jesse's silly rhymes.'

'It's a deal!' thought Samuel. And there and then, he poured some oil over David's head.

'That's it,' he said to Jesse. 'Now remember: don't tell Saul what I've done, or I'll be on the run. Oh, no! I've got to get out of here, before it gets me completely!'

As Samuel set of down the road he thought, 'David seems a strange choice. Still, there's one thing – he doesn't make up poetry. I wonder which one of them does.'

Our Story

Draw attention to the display; explain which examples are real and which imaginary and again see whether the other children can think of any more. Let them learn not to take things simply at face value.

Prayers

We're Sad

We're sorry, God,
for being unfair to people.
We jump to conclusions about them
just because of their appearance,
Please forgive us,
and help us to be fair.

We're Glad

Thank you, God, for wonderful surprises
when people turn out differently
from the way we expect.
Thank you for making the world
so unpredictable!

Let's Pray for People

Some people get badly treated,
just because they look different.
Please, God, help them to know
that you love them all,
and help us to control our prejudice.

Songs

God is making a wonderful world (WUW)
I'm black, I'm white, I'm short, I'm tall (WUW)
Stand up! Walk tall! (WW)
The best gift (CAP)

Appearances Can Be Deceptive
God's Story

Narrator	Long ago, God had a job for Samuel the prophet.
God	Samuel, I want you to go and see Jesse at Bethlehem and anoint one of his sons as king.
Samuel	Bethlehem? Nothing important happens in Bethlehem.
God	My Word! You ain't seen nothin' yet!
Samuel	Pardon?
God	That's my favourite quotation, but it's after your time.
Samuel	Can we just get back to this Bethlehem thing?
God	Just go – I'll tell you which one to anoint.
Narrator	So Samuel turned up at Jesse's house one afternoon.
Jesse	Hello, hello, hello, It's good old Sam the prophet man! Have you come with some message of doom?
Samuel	Look Jesse, I just say what God's given me to say, so if you want to moan at anybody, you'd better talk to him.
Jesse	Silly bloke – can't take a joke!
Narrator	The trouble was that Jesse fancied himself as a bit of a poet – why, no one could understand, although it was said that one of his sons was a bit of a song writer.
Samuel	Just send for your family and we'll get started.
Jesse	All right, Sammy, keep your wig on; how'd I know there's something big on?
Narrator	Jesse's sons got ready for the celebration.

- They *washed their faces*
- and they *cleaned their teeth*
- and they *combed their hair*

Narrator	Samuel was really pleased when the first son arrived.
God	Don't go by his appearance. I look at the heart.
Samuel	Oh, his heart'll be fine – healthy looking chap.
God	Don't get clever with me. You know what I mean.
Narrator	The next one to arrive was Abinadab.
Jesse	This is my son – another one.
Samuel	*(Aside)* I've got to get out of here! Where's my oil?
God	Not so fast, sonny! This is not the one.
Jesse	This one is Shammah – takes after his mamma.
Narrator	How long was this going to go on for! Altogether, Jesse presented seven sons to Samuel.
Samuel	Have you got any more?
Jesse	Yes, there's another – he's their baby brother. He's not like the rest – you've looked at the best. I let him earn his keep by caring for the sheep. Here he is.
David	Hello, I'm David.
Samuel	Thank the Lord! He's not a jumped up amateur poet!
Narrator	David was young – and didn't look at all like a king.
God	That's the one! Don't just sit there, get the oil out.
Narrator	Samuel poured some oil over David's head.
Samuel	Well, that's it, Jesse. Don't tell Saul what I've done, or I'll be on the run. Oh, no! I've got to get out of here!
Narrator	With that, Samuel set off away from Jesse's farm.
Samuel	Well, there's one thing about David – he doesn't make up poetry. I wonder which one of them does.

Whose Baby?

Based on 1 Kings 3:16-28

BEFORE THE DAY

Play 'Call My Bluff!' Think of something the children have done together, such as a class outing, and get one or a group of them to describe it. Ask another individual or group to make up a different (but plausible) account of it. Have both versions written down and let each group choose someone to present it to the assembly.

• Think about the actions for all the children to join in during the story.

ON THE DAY

Introduction

In a little while, there'll be a game for us all to play, but first we're going to say our 'Thank you' prayer.

'Thank you' Prayer

Thank you, God, for all you give us,
thank you for the earth and sea;
thank you, God, for special people,
thank you, God, for making me.

God's Story

Becky and Sally were flatmates, but they didn't like one another. As it happened, they were both expecting babies.

'I bet mine will be better looking than yours,' said Becky to Sally.

'Well, mine will be brainier because you've always been stupid,' answered Sally.

Becky's baby was born first. It was a beautiful little boy. Sally looked at him and said, 'Ugh! He's all red and wrinkled!'

'All children are like that to start with,' said Becky, crossly. 'But the wrinkles go after a few days. Why didn't yours?'

'Now, you two,' said the midwife, 'can't you stop quarrelling even at a time like this?'

'I don't care what you say,' Sally grumbled. 'My baby won't be red and wrinkled!' But he was. People used to come round and admire the babies, but Becky and Sally always tried to score points off one another. 'Of course, my baby has nicer eyes than hers,' Becky would say, and Sally would answer, 'Mine's ever so good you know – he hardly ever cries.'

One morning, Becky woke up and had a terrible shock. Her baby was dead. Becky screamed and cried.

But then she looked a little closer and realised it wasn't her baby. She rushed over to Sally's crib and there, sure enough, was her baby alive and well.

If she hadn't been so angry, Becky might have felt sorry for Sally – even though she didn't like her at all – but as it was she was just plain furious! 'You give me back my baby!' she yelled.

'You're mad!' said Sally. 'That's my baby.'

There was only one thing for it. They would have to get the law on it.

King Solomon was just finishing his breakfast when he heard the commotion at the palace gates. 'Really!' he said, in a fed up sort of voice. 'Can't a royal person even have his breakfast in peace?' He was a good king, though, so he put on his official clothes and went down to the palace gate. He always settled quarrels in public, so that everybody could see he was being fair and there were no more arguments about it.

When Solomon got to the gate, Becky and Sally were still hard at it.

'Give me my baby, you ugly little witch!' shouted Becky.

'Yours took one look at you and died of fright!' yelled Sally.

'Be quiet,' said Solomon, 'or I'll have you both locked up until you calm down. Now, what's all the fuss about?' Both women started to shout and argue again, and Solomon had to separate them. 'You first,' he said to Becky.

'It's like this,' said Becky, 'We both had babies and when I woke up this morning mine was dead. Then I realised that Prune-face here . . .'

'Don't you call me Prune-face, Banana-legs!' shouted Sally.

'One more word from you and I'll really lock you up!' said the king. 'Now, Becky, just tell me the story without any silly insults.'

'She swapped them,' said Becky. 'The live baby's mine and the dead one's hers.'

'She's lying,' screamed Sally. 'He's my baby.'

Of course, Solomon didn't know which he was, but he thought he might be able to find out. 'Get me a sword,' he said, and the whole crowd went deathly quiet. What was he going to do? 'We can't decide whose he is,' he said, 'so I'm going to cut him in two and you can have half each.'

'You can't do that!' Becky wailed.

Sally thought, 'At least then her baby will be dead a well as mine.' So she said, 'Sounds fair to me – give us half each.' Sally really was a nasty person, but Becky was no angel either even though she was right in this particular case.

The servant put the baby on a table, and another lifted the sword high above the baby. Becky couldn't stand it any more. 'Give him to her!' she shouted. 'I'd rather give him away than have him killed.'

Solomon gently handed the baby over to Becky. 'I can tell you're his mother,' he said. 'Take him home and look after him.'

Becky was thrilled.

- She *picked the baby up*
- she *rocked him in her arms*
- she *hugged him close*

One of Solomon's servants said to him, 'Your Majesty, you wouldn't really have cut that baby up, would you?'

'Of course not,' said Solomon, 'but it did the trick. You see, when you really love someone, you'd rather let them go than have them hurt. So I knew she was the real mother.'

Our Story

Get the two groups of children to present their stories, and then ask the whole assembly to vote for one or other as being correct. You could make it more fun, space permitting, by asking the children to move to one or other side of the hall. When the result has been announced, you can point out that we aren't all a clever as Solomon. Sometimes people get it wrong and unfair things happen. That's why honesty's so important.

Prayers

We're Sad

Sometimes we can be so selfish, or so angry
that we don't think straight.
Then innocent people get hurt,
and we end up unhappy as well.
Please God, help us to understand
that true happiness often means letting go.

We're Glad

Thank you, God, for wise people
who know how to get to the truth.
Thank you also for people who are so loving
that they would rather lose
than see innocents hurt.
Please teach us all to love unselfishly.

Let's Pray for People

We pray for people who make themselves
and other people unhappy
because they are selfish or angry.
Help us all to learn to let go
even of the most precious things
when it is the loving thing to do.

Songs

Out to the great wide world we go! (WUW)
Love is his word (A)
Let there be peace on earth (A)
A better world (A)
God knows me (CAP)
He's got the whole world in his hands (CAP)
If I had a hammer (CAP)

Whose Baby?
God's Story

Narrator	Becky and Sally were both expecting babies. They were flatmates, but they hated one another.
Becky	I bet mine will be better looking than yours.
Sally	Mine will be brainier; you've always been stupid.
Narrator	See what I mean? They couldn't be nice to one another even if their lives depended on it. Becky's baby was born first. It was a beautiful little boy.
Sally	Ugh! He's all red and wrinkled – what an ugly child!
Becky	All children are like that to start with, but the wrinkles go after a few days. Why didn't yours?
Narrator	Sally's baby was born a few days later, and he was lovely – but Becky and Sally still couldn't be friends.
Becky	Of course, my baby has nicer eyes than yours.
Sally	Mine's ever so good you know – he hardly ever cries.
Narrator	One morning, Becky woke up and had a terrible shock. Her baby was very pale, and very cold, and he wasn't breathing. He was dead. Becky cried.
Sally	Hey, I'm trying to sleep. Beautiful women like me need their sleep – it makes no difference to you.
Narrator	Becky looked a little closer and realised it wasn't her baby. She rushed over to Sally's crib and there, sure enough, was her child alive and well.
Becky	You give me back my baby!
Sally	You're mad! Anyone can see that that's my baby.
Narrator	Then they started screaming and shouting at each other. There was only one thing for it. They would have to get the law on it. King Solomon was just finishing his breakfast when he heard the commotion outside.

Solomon	Really! Can't a royal person even have his breakfast in peace? Be quiet, or I'll have you both locked up until you calm down. Now what's it all about? You first.
Becky	We both had babies and when I woke up this morning mine was dead. Then I realised that Prune-face here . . .
Sally	Don't you call me Prune-face, Banana-legs!
Solomon	One more word from you and I'll lock you up. Now, Becky, just tell me the story without any silly insults.
Becky	She swapped them. The live baby's mine.
Solomon	Your turn, Sally.
Sally	She's lying. He's my baby.
Solomon	Give me the baby. I'm going to cut him in two and you can have half each.
Becky	You can't cut my baby in half!
Sally	Sounds fair to me – give us half each.
Narrator	The servant put the baby on a table, and another took the sword. He lifted it up, high above the baby and waited for the king's command to cut the child in two.
Becky	Give him to her! Give him to her. I'd rather give him away than have him killed.
	• She *picked the baby up* • she rocked him in her arms • She *hugged him close*
Solomon	I can tell you're his mother, Becky. When you really love someone, you'd rather let them go than have them hurt. I wouldn't really have hurt him, of course.
Narrator	That was one reason why everybody said that Solomon was a very wise king indeed.

Elijah's Last Journeys

Based on 2 Kings 2:1-15

BEFORE THE DAY

Absent friends. Do the children have friends who have gone away? Have they themselves moved house/school and left friends behind? Write the friends' names up on a flipchart, leaving space to add others. If it is felt appropriate in the particular circumstances, this could also be an opportunity to talk sensitively about bereavement.

• Think about the actions for all the children to join in during the story.

ON THE DAY
Introduction
We'll hear a story soon about two friends who had to go separate ways. First, we're going to say our 'Thank you' prayer.

'Thank you' Prayer
Thank you, God, for all you give us,
thank you for the earth and sea;
thank you, God, for special people,
thank you, God, for making me.

God's Story
Elijah and Elisha were friends. Elijah was the chief prophet at the time, and Elisha was his pupil. Everyone guessed that God would probably ask Elisha to take over sometime.

One day, they both knew that it was going to happen. Elijah seemed restless.

'God wants me to go to Bethel,' said Elijah. 'You stay here and rest.'

'Not on your life!' answered Elisha. 'I want to be around when the action starts.'

'Well, all right, then,' grunted Elijah. 'Just make sure you keep up.' And he set off at a cracking pace toward Bethel. When they got there, they found a reception committee waiting for them. Some of them took Elisha aside and said, 'Did you know that God's going to take Elijah away, today?'

'Yes,' said Elisha, 'but don't tell him.'

Then Elisha sat down on a handy milestone and took his sandals off. 'My life!' he said. 'But can that man walk! I've got blisters where I didn't even know I'd got skin!'

Elijah came up to him and looked down at his feet for a moment. 'You young people!' he said. 'In my day we'd walk miles just to find a drink of water, and think nothing of it.' Then he smiled. 'Look, you stay here with these good people. I'm going to go to Jericho.'

'Whatever for?' exclaimed Elisha. Ever since Joshua's jam session, no one's dared throw a decent party in case something collapses. There's really nothing to go to in Jericho.'

Elijah was very patient. 'I've already said you can stay here,' he said.

'Not blooming likely!' said Elisha. 'I'm not leaving you today.'

So off they set, and Elijah didn't seem the least bit tired but went striding along ahead.

'What's the matter?' gasped Elisha. 'You're rushing around like there's no tomorrow.'

'Funny you should say that . . .' replied Elijah. And Elisha wished he hadn't.

At Jericho, there was another reception committee. One of them came up to Elisha. 'Sooth! Sooth!' he chanted.

'What d'you mean, "Sooth"?' snapped Elisha, impatiently.

'Sorry, Guv,' said the prophet, 'but I've got to say "Sooth" because I'm a "Sooth" sayer. D'you know your boss is leaving today?'

'Yes,' said Elisha, 'but don't tell to him. And don't go yelling "Sooth" in his ear, either – if you know what's good for you.'

• The man *raised his eyebrows*
• he *scratched his head*
• then he *rubbed his nose*

'Well!' he said. 'I've had my nose bitten off a few times, but that's what I call a mega bite!' And he went off, chuntering to himself.

Elisha sat down and looked mournfully at his feet. 'I've got blisters on my blisters, now!' he groaned.

'Oh, don't tell me about blisters, said Elijah.

When I was a young prophet...'

'I know, I know!' Elisha interrupted. 'Up to your neck in muck and...'

'No need to be offensive!' Elijah sniffed. 'Anyway, you can have a rest now, because I'm going to Jordan. You wait here.'

'Not on your cotton-picking life!' said Elisha. 'After all this walking, you're going to a nice cool, fresh river, and you think I'm staying here?'

So off they went, and soon they got to Jordan. That's right – another reception committee.

'D'you know...' one of them began.

'Oh, don't you start as well!' said Elisha. 'I know he's leaving today, and I'm unhappy enough without you rubbing it in. And talking of rubbing – Oh, my feet!'

'Sorry, I'm sure!' said the man, rather stiffly. Then Elijah came over and said, kindly, 'Sorry about all the walking, but we're about there now. Let's get across that water.'

Elijah took off his cloak and hit the water with it. There, before Elisha's astonished eyes, the water moved to each side and left a nice dry path to walk across. 'Come on,' said Elijah, 'or you'll miss the big moment.'

As they walked, Elijah said, 'Is there anything I can do for you before I go?'

Elisha was still amazed by what Elijah had just done. 'A double portion of whatever it is that you've got wouldn't go amiss!' he said.

'That's difficult,' said Elijah, 'but if you actually see me taken away, then you'll get your wish. So stick with me, kid – I'm going places.'

Elisha did exactly that, until suddenly he saw something bright and terrifying coming towards them. He did his best to stay close to Elijah, but the strange thing came rushing through between them and picked Elijah up. It was a horse and chariot which seemed to be made of fire! Up and up it went, carrying Elijah with it. As Elisha looked up in astonishment, he saw Elijah's cloak coming down from the chariot to land at his feet. He picked it up and put it on.

'That's it!' he thought. 'It's a sign!'

And it was. Elisha became a great prophet, just as Elijah had been.

Our Story

Explain about the names on the board, and invite the rest of the assembly to add others. Then offer a short prayer for the absent friends.

Prayers

We're Sad

Wonderful God,
We're not always like Elijah and Elisha.
Sometimes we let people down,
and we're not there when they need us.
We're sorry, God.
Help us to be better friends to each other.

We're Glad

God, our friend,
you're always here for us.
Even though we sometimes find it hard
to recognise you,
you never leave us on our own.
Thank you.

Let's Pray for People

Some people don't seem to have any real
  friends.
They have to get through the hard times
without the help they really need.
Make us alert to other people,
so that we recognise when they're lonely;
then we can be friends to them.

Songs

Keep on travelling on! (WUW)
Thank you, O God, for all our friends (WW)
Blowin' in the wind (A)
The journey of life (CAP)
One more step (CAP)
When I needed a neighbour (CAP)

Elijah's Last Journeys
God's Story

Narrator Elijah, who was the chief prophet, was training Elisha. Elijah was often restless, but on this particular day he *really* seemed to have sand in his underwear!

Elijah I'm going to Bethel. You stay here and have a rest.

Elisha And miss the action? Not likely! I'm coming with you.

Narrator When they arrived, they were met by a reception committee of priests and prophets.

1st Prophet Do you know God's going to take Elijah away, today?

Elisha Yes, but don't tell him. Gosh, can that man walk! I've got blisters where I didn't even know I'd got skin!

Elijah Look, you rest here. I'm going to go to Jericho.

Elisha Why? Nothing ever happens in Jericho. Ever since Joshua brought the walls down, no one's dared throw a party in case something collapses. Oh, all right – I'm coming.

Narrator Elijah didn't seem at all tired but went striding ahead.

Narrator In Jericho, they found another reception committee; this time from the Prophets' Commission, Department Of Soothsaying.

2nd Prophet Sooth! Sooth!

Elisha *(Impatiently)* What d'you mean, 'Sooth'?

2nd Prophet Sorry, Guv, but I've got to say 'Sooth' because I'm a 'Sooth' sayer. Your boss is going away today.

Elisha Well, don't go yelling 'Sooth' in his ear – or else.

Narrator	The soothsayer looked hurt.

- He *raised his eyebrows*
- he *scratched his head*
- then he *rubbed his nose*

2nd Prophet	Well! I've had my nose bitten off a few times, but that's what I call a mega bite!
Elijah	I'm going to Jordan, Elisha. You wait here.
Elisha	Not on your life! I'm coming, so I can soak these feet!
Narrator	So they went. This time the reception committee was from the Prophets' Bureau.
3rd Prophet	Did you know ..
Elisha	Oh, don't you start as well! Oh, my feet!
3rd Prophet	Sorry, I'm sure!
Elijah	Sorry about all the walking, but we're about there now.
Narrator	Elijah hit the water with his cloak. There, to Elisha's amazement, the water moved aside and left a dry path.
Elijah	Come on, or you'll miss the big moment. Is there anything I can do for you before I go?
Elisha	Well, I'd like a double portion of whatever it is that you've got.
Elijah	I'll tell you what. If you see me taken away, then you'll get it. So stick with me, kid – I'm going places.
Narrator	Suddenly, a horse and chariot which seemed to be made of fire came rushing through between them and carried Elijah off. As Elisha watched he saw Elijah's cloak coming down to land at his feet. Elisha became a great prophet, and all the people said how like Elijah he was.

Room at the Top

Based on 2 Kings 4:8-17

BEFORE THE DAY

How many different ways can the children think of by which to show friendship? Would they share their chocolate, let their friends join in their games, or write to them when they're ill. Get them to design a motorway-style 'services' sign with symbols for the different ideas.

• Think about the actions for all the children to join in during the story.

ON THE DAY

Introduction

In a little while, we'll be thinking about friendship. First, we're going to say our 'Thank you' prayer.

'Thank you' Prayer

Thank you, God, for all you give us,
thank you for the earth and sea;
thank you, God, for special people,
thank you, God, for making me.

God's Story

This story is about a woman whose name no one knows. She's usually called 'the Shunemite woman', because she lived in Shunem, but we're going to call her Deborah.

Deborah was a very important woman. Now some people who seem as important as that aren't very nice, but Deborah was a lovely person. One day she saw a man walking past who looked as though he could do with a rest and a good meal. So Deborah went over and said, 'Hello, you're a stranger round here, aren't you?'

'That's right,' the man answered. 'My name's Elisha. I travel around quite a bit, but this is my first visit to Shunem.'

'Well, you're very welcome,' Deborah told him. 'Would you like to come in?'

'Oh, no, thank you very much all the same,' answered Elisha. 'I've travelled a long way, and I'm afraid my coat isn't very clean. I wouldn't want to mess up your nice furniture.'

'That doesn't matter in the slightest,' Deborah assured him. 'I have someone who comes in three times a week to clean, and he may as well earn his wages.'

'Well, it really is very kind of you,' said Elisha, 'but I'm sure you've got important things to do.'

'Nonsense!' exclaimed Deborah. 'What could be more important than sharing a meal with a nice person like you. You must have some wonderful tales to tell if you travel about as much as you say.'

'I must admit, I've seen a thing or two,' mused Elisha, 'like that time my best friend got carried away in a flying chariot.'

'Now that I really must hear!' exclaimed Deborah, and she took Elisha by the arm and led him into her house.

'This is beautiful,' said Elisha. 'I really can't sit on those lovely cushions with these clothes on.'

'Well, I don't think you'd better take them off,' laughed Deborah. 'Go on – sit down!'

While Elisha was there, Deborah's husband came in. We don't know his name, either, so we'll call him Bart. He and Elisha got on like a house on fire, and soon it was as though they had all known each other for years. Elisha often visited Shunem after that, and he always called on Bart and Deborah.

One day, Deborah said to Bart, 'I think there's more to Elisha than meets the eye. I think he's some sort of prophet or holy man.'

'You could be right,' Bart replied. 'He seems very wise as well as kind.'

'I think we ought to build a spare room,' said Deborah. 'Then Elisha can stay here in comfort.'

'Well, I don't know where we're going to build an extra room,' said Bart. 'The garden's not very big, and we've already taken up part of it with that little garage for the chariot.'

Deborah couldn't think at first, either. She really wanted to do it, but she knew Bart was right. There wasn't any room. Then one day she had a bit of time to herself and decided to do a spot of sunbathing. She could have a nice snooze while she was at it. So she settled down in the garden, sat back and closed her eyes.

It was no good; every time Deborah began to doze off, someone would pass by and call out 'Hello!'

Then she had an idea. 'If I were up on the flat roof, she thought, 'no one would be able to see me.' So she went and got a ladder and propped it against the side of the house. It was very nice on the roof, but a little uncomfortable, so after a while Deborah went down for a deck chair which she hauled up to the roof using a rope. Before long, she'd got a footstool, a little table with a cool drink on it, two or three cushions and a sunshade, and she was really comfortable. She lay back in her deck chair and started to doze off.

Then just as she was falling asleep, she heard a voice! But this time it was her own thoughts she was hearing. 'Why not build a room for Elisha up here?' the thought said. Deborah was so excited she forgot about sunbathing and went rushing out to find Bart, who had gone to market.

'You'll never believe it,' she told him. 'I was just lying on the roof . . .'

'You were what?' said Bart, astonished.

'Lying on the roof,' answered Deborah. 'Doesn't everybody?'

When Bart got over his amazement, he thought Deborah's idea was a very good one. So they called in a builder.

- The builder *drew some plans*
- and *built some walls*
- and *hammered in some nails*

Soon there was a lovely little guest room on the roof.

Next time Elisha came, they showed him that he had his own special room.

'I don't know how to thank you,' he said.

'No need,' said Deborah. We just love having you to stay.'

'There must be something I can do,' Elisha insisted. 'Perhaps I'll put a good word in for you with the king.'

'Don't be silly,' laughed Deborah. 'I know him like my own brother. The only thing we want, nobody can give us. Unless you've got a spare child hidden in your luggage, just forget it. We love having you here and you don't have to repay us.'

'Ah!' exclaimed Elisha. 'So that's what you want. Well, by this time next year, you will have a lovely little baby boy in your arms. You've got God's word for that.'

And Elisha was absolutely right. But that's another story.

Our Story

Explain to the assembly what the sign is generally about, and then see whether they can interpret the specific symbols. Would they want to add anything else?

Prayers

We're Sad

Sometimes we're so wrapped up in our own problems
that we don't notice what other people need.
It's not that we mean to be unkind;
we just don't notice them.
Please forgive us, God,
and make us more aware of others.

We're Glad

Thank you, God, for all the different people
you send our way.
Thank you for the different things
we can learn from each of them,
and the friendships we can have with them.

Let's Pray for People

We pray for people who help others.
Help them to know that what they do
is noticed and appreciated.
Show us what we can do to support them.

Songs

Keep on travelling on! (WUW)
Out to the great wide world we go! (WUW)
Thank you, O God, for all our friends (WW)
Magic penny (A)
Love is his word (A)
One more step (CAP)
When I needed a neighbour (CAP)
The best gift (CAP)

Room at the Top
God's Story

Narrator   Deborah was an important woman who lived in Shunem. One day she saw a man walking past who looked as though he could do with a rest and a good meal.

Deborah   Hello, you're a stranger round here, aren't you?

Elisha   Yes; my name's Elisha. This is my first visit here.

Deborah   Would you like to come in and have some food?

Elisha   Well, it's very kind of you, but I wouldn't want to be any trouble, and you must have important things to do.

Deborah   Nonsense! You must have some wonderful tales to tell from your travels.

Elisha   I've certainly seen a thing or two. There was that time my best friend got carried away by some flying horses.

Deborah   Now that I really must hear! Come on in.

Narrator   While Elisha was there, Deborah's husband, Bart, came in. He and Elisha got on like a house on fire, and Elisha often visited them after that.

Deborah   You know, Bart, I think Elisha might be a prophet.

Bart   You could be right.

Deborah   I think we ought to build a spare room for him.

Bart   Well, I don't know. We haven't much space.

Narrator   Deborah went and sat outside to think quietly. It *should* have been very peaceful in the garden.

Neighbour   Hello, Deborah, having a nice rest?

Deborah   *(Patiently)* No, but I'd like to.

Narrator	It was no good, though. Every time anyone walked past, they called out and disturbed her. So to get a bit of peace, she went and got a ladder and climbed up onto the roof. Peace at last – then she had an idea!
Deborah	That's it! Why not build a room for Elisha up here?
Narrator	Deborah was so excited she forgot about sunbathing rushed off to find Bart, who had gone to market.
Deborah	You'll never believe it – I was just lying on the roof . . .
Bart	You were what?
Deborah	Lying on the roof. Doesn't everybody?
Narrator	Bart liked Deborah's idea and called in a builder.

- The builders *drew some plans*
- and *built some walls*
- and *hammered in some nails*

And soon Elisha had a lovely little room on the roof.

Elisha	I don't know how to thank you.
Deborah	No need. We love having you to stay.
Elisha	There must be something I can do. Perhaps I'll put a good word in for you with the king.
Deborah	Don't be silly! I know him like my own brother. The only thing we want, nobody can give us. Unless you're hiding a spare child in your luggage, just forget it. We love having you here and you don't have to repay us.
Elisha	Ah! So that's what you want. Well, by this time next year, you will have a lovely little baby boy in your arms. You've got God's word for that.
Narrator	And Elisha was absolutely right. But that's another story.

Life's Like That!

Based on 2 Kings 4:18-37

BEFORE THE DAY

This story is an opportunity to explore the fact that we don't always get what we deserve, but it works both ways – we get good things as well as bad. Let the children draw some examples of both, e.g. people suffering the effects of floods or gales, lottery winners receiving their (unearned) cheques, sports matches being rained off, beautiful weather at the seaside, etc. Put the pictures up in a display, not in separate categories but randomly mixed.

• Think about the actions for all the children to join in during the story.

ON THE DAY

Introduction

The world doesn't seem to be a very fair place, and we're going to think about that in a few minutes. First, we're going to say our 'Thank you' prayer.

'Thank you' Prayer

Thank you, God, for all you give us,
thank you for the earth and sea;
thank you, God, for special people,
thank you, God, for making me.

God's Story

Deborah, the Shunemite woman who was a friend of Elisha, was really worried. Her husband, Bart, seemed bad-tempered and unreasonable. He he made some very unkind remarks about her cooking – just because she was trying out a few new recipes of her own.

Bart, of course, had his own version of the story to tell, and he told it to his next door neighbour, Luke. 'I don't know what's got into her!' he said one day. 'Last week, the only food she would cook was figs and onions. We had them on toast for breakfast, and then in an omelette for lunch, followed by figs and onions in chocolate sauce for dessert.'

'Well, there's one thing,' Luke laughed. 'It can't get any worse!'

'Oh can't it!' answered Bart. 'That's what you know. This week it was stewed oranges in camel meat stock. I'm not kidding you, my stomach's not been right for weeks!'

Luke thought he had the answer.

• He *scratched his head*
• and he *stroked his beard*
• and he *frowned very wisely*

'She needs help,' he said, looking very wise. 'She's obviously having a breakdown. You wouldn't understand the details, but take it from me – that's what she's having.'

Bart didn't like to ask any more questions, since Luke was now looking very knowledgeable and superior, and Bart was sure he really ought to understand all this – but just then they heard a very worrying sound.

It was the sound of laughter. Shrieking, uncontrollable, hysterical laughter. 'Terribly sorry, old man,' said Luke. 'Sounds like a really serious case to me.'

'That's not Deborah,' Bart said. 'That's coming from your house.'

Sure enough, just inside Luke's kitchen window was his wife, Sandy, with tears streaming down her face, and laughing fit to bust! 'You pair of silly, pompous men!' she gasped in between peals of laughter. 'Deborah's not ill – she's pregnant!'

"Don't be silly!' answered Luke. 'What would you know about it?'

'Well, I've been there myself five times,' giggled Sandy, 'which is five times more than both of you put together. You should know that women often fancy strange food when we're pregnant.'

Sandy was absolutely right. Elisha had promised Deborah and Bart a child, and it was actually happening!

And what a baby it was! A lovely little boy whom they named Tom. He grew up into a strong, sturdy child who liked striding around the fields with his Dad. He very quickly learned all about caring for the land and growing crops. Everybody loved Tom very much, and especially Elisha who always played with him on his visits.

One day, out in the fields, Tom started feeling ill. Soon, he had a raging headache and the whole world seemed to be spinning round. 'I'm not feeling very well' he said.

Bart asked one of the farm hands to take him back to the house. Poor Deborah did all she could, but it was no use. Tom was a lot more sick than anyone had realised, and he just got worse and worse until he died.

Deborah was beside herself with grief and anger. She took Tom upstairs into the special room she'd had built and laid him on Elisha's bed, and then she got on a donkey and went out to find the prophet. He went to meet her and gave her a hug.

'Why did you do this? Deborah asked. 'Why did your God give us a child, just to make us unhappy by taking him away?'

Elisha was horrified! 'Let's go to your house!' he said. They hurried off, and when they arrived Elisha went up to his room and found Tom's body on his bed. After he had prayed he picked Tom up and hugged him. Tom's body started to get warm again. Elisha put him down on the bed and prayed again, and then he picked him up and hugged him again, and this time he could just feel a little heart beating away against him. Then Tom's eyes opened and he said, 'Oh, hello! When did you get here?'

Elisha went to the door and opened it. When Deborah saw Tom alive, she started crying all over again, but this time it was with happiness!

Deborah and Bart hugged Tom and thanked Elisha.

'Don't thank me,' said Elisha. 'It's God that's done this. He doesn't break his word. And he doesn't play around with people's feelings, either.'

Our Story

Look at the pictures and point out that none of those people have deserved what has happened – to some extent, life's a lottery! Explain that the pictures are randomly placed, because happy and sad things often seem to be mixed up together in life, as well. How does this affect our attitudes to people who have had a raw deal from life?

Prayers

We're Sad

Sometimes, we don't understand
why other people are angry,
and we get angry in return
when we should be listening.
Please forgive us, God,
and help us to be better friends.

We're Glad

Thank you, God, for people like Elisha,
who really care about other people.
Thank you for patient people, who understand
when others say things they don't mean.
Thank you, God, for wonderful friends.

Let's Pray for People

Sometimes dreadful, unfair things happen.
Sometimes people who don't deserve it get hurt.
Please, God, give them friends who understand,
who will listen to what they need to say
even when it's hurtful.

Songs

Thank you, O God, for all our friends (WW)
Love is his word (A)
The best gift (CAP)
When I needed a neighbour (CAP)

Life's Like That!

God's Story

Narrator   Deborah, the Shunemite woman who was a friend of Elisha, was really worried about her husband, Bart. He seemed to be very bad-tempered and unreasonable, and was most unkind about her cooking. But Bart saw things differently, and said so to their neighbour.

Bart   I don't know what's got into her, Luke! Last week, the only food she would cook was figs and onions.

Luke   Figs and onions! You're having me on!

Bart   Would I joke about something as serious as my dinner? Before that, it was stewed oranges in camel meat stock. My stomach's not been right for weeks!

Narrator   Luke thought he had the answer.

- He *scratched his head*
- and he *stroked his beard*
- and he *frowned very wisely*

Luke   She's having some sort of breakdown.

Bart   Some sort of what?

Luke   Oh, it's very technical. You wouldn't understand – I don't think we'll really understand it for thousands of years yet, but that's what she's having all right.

Narrator   Bart didn't like to ask any more questions, since Luke was now looking very knowledgeable and superior. Just then, though, they heard the sound of shrieking, uncontrollable, hysterical laughter.

Luke   Terribly sorry, old man. Sounds like a serious case.

Bart   That's coming from *your* house. It's *your* wife.

Narrator	Bart was right. Just inside the kitchen window was Luke's wife, Sandy, doubled up, with tears streaming down her face, and laughing fit to bust!
Sandy	You silly, pompous men! Deborah's pregnant!
Luke	Don't be silly, Sandy! What would you know about it?
Sandy	Well, I've been there myself five times, which is five times more than both of you put together. You should know that women often fancy strange foods when we're pregnant.
Narrator	Poor Luke felt nearly as silly as he looked – but it would have been impossible to have felt *that* silly!
Bart	What a relief! So we aren't falling out of love, after all! Elisha promised us a child, and we're having one!
Narrator	Soon, they had a lovely little boy whom they named Tom. He grew very strong and healthy for a few years, but then for no apparent reason he died. Deborah was beside herself with grief and anger, and went to find Elisha.
Deborah	Why did you do this? We'd got used to not having a child. Why did your God give us one, just to make us unhappy by taking him away?
Elisha	Let's go to your house!
Narrator	They hurried off, and when they arrived Elisha went up to his room and found Tom's body on his bed. As he prayed, and hugged Tom, a wonderful thing happened. Tom's body started to get warm again, and soon his eyes opened. He really was alive!
Elisha	Deborah, Bart, you can come in now – he's fine.
Deborah	This is wonderful! How can we ever thank you?
Elisha	Don't thank me. It's God that's done this. He doesn't break his word. And he doesn't play around with people's feelings, either.

Keep It Simple
Based on 2 Kings 5:1-14

BEFORE THE DAY

Get the children to use their imaginations and design outlandish, complicated versions of simply everyday objects: a tooth cleaning machine with lots of rotary brushes and toothpaste dispensers attached to robotic arms around a chair; a tin-opener made from a hacksaw mounted on a stand, with jigs for holding the tins still and magnets for removing the severed lids; an alarm clock operated by water dripping steadily into a container – when the water level is just right, a series of rubber balls run down a tube to land on the skin of a drum. The more outlandish and complicated the devices are, the better!

- Think about the actions for all the children to join in during the story.

ON THE DAY

Introduction

We've got some interesting new inventions to look at shortly, but first we're going to say our 'Thank you' prayer.

'Thank you' Prayer

Thank you, God, for all you give us,
thank you for the earth and sea;
thank you, God, for special people,
thank you, God, for making me.

God's Story

Naaman lived in the country of Aram, and was a commander in the king's army. He was a great soldier who had been involved in lots of battles and had the scars to prove it, but when he wasn't soldiering he lived quietly with his wife, Jessica, in their house near the barracks.

Naaman and his army were often sent by the king of Aram to raid Israel and bring back treasure. The king wasn't really such a bad man; kings just thought they could do that kind of thing in those days, and a lot of rulers and politicians still haven't learnt any better, now.

Anyway, on one of the raids Naaman brought back a young girl called Anna and gave her to his wife as a slave. Now you might have thought that Anna would hate Naaman and Jessica for that, but she always tried not to. 'After all,' she used to say, 'we've all got to live together and hating them would just make me feel even more unhappy.' So although she missed her home very much, and longed to go back, she always tried to think kindly of Nathan and Jessica and to be helpful.

- She *dusted their furniture*
- she *cooked their food (stirring action)*
- she *chopped wood for the fire*

One day, Anna said to Jessica, 'I hope you won't mind my saying this, my Lady, but the commander doesn't seem very well. That nasty rash is getting worse.'

It was true. Nathan had a really uncomfortable skin disease, and it seemed to be spreading, but none of the doctors in Aram could do anything about it. 'I know someone who can, though,' said Anna.' Send him to Israel to meet the prophet who lives there, and he'll make the commander well again.'

When the king of Aram heard about it he thought it was certainly worth a try, so he sent Naaman to the king of Israel with a letter, saying, 'Please make my army commander better.'

'Oh dear,' groaned the king of Israel. 'He's trying to pick a quarrel with me – how on earth can I make this soldier better?' And he got really frightened.

Well, you know how rumours about royal families spread – before long the whole country was talking about how frightened the king was, and wondering if it meant the end of the monarchy.

'It's true, you know,' someone said in the market place. 'He's so frightened he never goes to sleep any more. What sort of a king is he?'

Standing nearby was a man called Elisha. He was the prophet Anna had meant, but that's the trouble with some people: they think only kings and queens have the answers to anything – so Naaman had been sent to the wrong person! Still, it wasn't too late. Elisha sent a message to the king of Israel, saying, 'Send Naaman to me – I'll help him, and then you can get a good night's sleep.'

So it was that Naaman turned up at Elisha's door. When Elisha opened it, Naaman stood and waited for something spectacular to happen; you know, a flashing light, or something, or perhaps God would zap him and make him fall over. He liked a bit of theatre, did Naaman. But all Elisha said was, 'Oh, it's you. Right. Go and take a dip in the river Jordan. In fact, while you're at it, take seven – you've had a long journey. Then you'll get rid of your rash.'

Well! What a let down! Naaman got back on his horse, and set off for home. He was furious! 'I'm not being made a fool of by any Israelite!' he said, but his servant was actually a lot wiser than him – which is often the case.

'Why not do it?' the servant asked, 'After all, if he'd asked you to do something difficult you'd have done it, just to get a bit of glory – so why not do something simple?'

It seemed like a good point. Anyway, Naaman was hot and sticky, and covered in dust, so he thought he might just give it a try. He stopped on the river bank and took off his clothes while his servant kept watch. Then he went into the river and ducked under. 'Ugh!' he thought, 'What do they empty into the river around here?' But he didn't want to look like a coward, so he went under seven times, just as he'd been told. Then he got out of the water and started to dry himself. 'There!' he said to his servant. 'Satisfied now? Let's go home before I have to do anything else that's stupid . . . What on earth's the matter with you now?'

His servant was staring at him as though he'd seen a ghost. 'Sir! Sir!' he shouted. 'Your rash has gone!' Naaman looked down, and sure enough, it had! His skin looked fresh and healthy again – almost like a baby's skin.

Naaman went rushing back to see Elisha and say thank you to him. He offered Elisha presents – beautiful clothes, gold and silver – but Elisha wouldn't accept any of them. That wasn't why he had helped Naaman. So Naaman set out for home, and thought what a lot he had learned during his visit to Israel.

When Naaman got home, everybody celebrated. Jessica was overjoyed to see Naaman looking so healthy, and not scratching himself all the time, and Anna was really pleased to see how happy they both were.

Naaman thanked Anna, and he thanked his servant, too. 'I'll never be too proud to do something simple again,' he said. 'Very often, the simplest ideas are really the best ones.'

Our Story

Show the whole group the designs, and let them have a bit of fun working out how they function, or even what they are. Then show them the everyday versions of them. Be careful to keep the atmosphere light-hearted so the children who did the designs can enjoy the fun and not feel ridiculed. Congratulate them on the ingenuity of their ideas.

Prayers

We're Sad

Loving God,
sometimes we're so proud!
Forgive us for being snobbish,
and show us how you work
in simple ways.

We're Glad

Thank you, God,
for the simple things in life:
for smiles, and hugs,
and for friendship.

Let's Pray for People

Let's pray for busy people;
people whose lives are so complicated
that they don't have time for simple beauty,
or for little joys.
Please help us make space in our own lives,
so that we can show how much those things
    matter.

Songs

God is making a wonderful world (WUW)
Out to the great wide world we go! (WUW)
Water of life (CAP)
He's got the whole world in his hand (CAP)
Morning has broken (CAP)

Keep It Simple
God's Story

Narrator   Naaman lived in the country of Aram, and was a commander in the king's army. Naaman and his army were often sent by the king of Aram to raid Israel and bring back treasure. On one of the raids Naaman brought back a young girl called Anna as a slave for his wife, Jessica.

Anna   Now you might have thought that I would hate Naaman and Jessica for that, but I always tried not to. After all, we've all got to live together and hating them would just make me feel even more unhappy. So I tried to be a good servant to them.

- I *dusted their furniture*
- I *cooked their food (stirring action)*
- and I *chopped wood for the fire*

Narrator   One day, Anna noticed something very worrying about Naaman, and spoke to Jessica about it.

Anna   I hope you won't mind me saying this, my Lady, but the commander doesn't seem very well. That nasty rash is getting worse. I think you should send him to the prophet who lives in Israel, and he'll cure him.

Narrator   The king of Aram thought it was certainly worth a try, so he sent Naaman to the king of Israel with a letter saying, 'Please make my army commander better.' The king of Israel thought Naaman's king was trying to pick a quarrel with him. How could he make anyone better? He got really frightened. And then – well, you know how rumours about royal families spread – before long the whole country was talking about it, and wondering if it meant the end of the monarchy. But Naaman should have gone to Elisha.

Elisha	Why do people think only kings and queens have the answers to anything? Send him to me.
Narrator	A bit later, Naaman knocked on Elisha's door.
Elisha	Oh, it's you. Go and take seven dips in the river.
Naaman	Is that it? I didn't come here to be made a fool of.
Narrator	Fortunately, as is often the case, Naaman's servant was actually a lot wiser than he was.
Servant	If he'd asked you to do something difficult you'd have done it, just to show off – so why not do this?
Naaman	I suppose so. Anyway, it's hot and I fancy a swim.
Narrator	So Naaman took off his clothes and jumped in.
Naaman	Ugh! What do they empty into the river around here?
Narrator	But Naaman didn't want to look like a wimp – so he went under seven times, just as he'd been told. Then he got out of the water and started to dry himself.
Naaman	There! Satisfied now?
Servant	Sir! Sir! Your rash has gone!
Naaman	Well, well! So it has. How amazing!
Servant	Very often, the simplest ideas are really the best ones.
Naaman	That's funny – Anna's always saying that, and I've only just realised how true it is. I should listen to my servants more. You know, you're quite a philosopher.
Servant	I've been called some names in my time, but really!

Live Connections

Based on Ezekiel 37:1-14

BEFORE THE DAY

Let the children help gather together a collection of simple musical instruments – tambourines, recorders etc., and recruit some volunteers to demonstrate them. They do not need to perform, but simply blow or hit the instruments to produce a noise; however, if you can do something more ambitious, why not?

• Think about the actions for all the children to join in during the story.

ON THE DAY

Introduction

This morning, we're going to celebrate being alive! But first, let's say our 'Thank you' prayer.

'Thank you' Prayer

Thank you, God, for all you give us,
thank you for the earth and sea;
thank you, God, for special people,
thank you, God, for making me.

God's Story

Hello, there! My name's Ezekiel, but you can call me Zeek if you like. I'm going to tell you about a really amazing dream that I had. Well, I say it was a dream – more of a vision, really, because God taught me something very important through it.

It was at the time when everybody in Israel had given up hope. I don't know why, but for some strange reason the whole world seemed to be against Israel. Every tuppenny-ha'penny dictator within a thousand miles seemed to want to have a go at us. It had got to the stage where a lot of people had left and gone to live elsewhere, and others had been taken away to be slaves. Some of the beautiful towns looked absolutely horrible – all derelict buildings and people crying in the streets. Really depressing it was, I don't mind telling you. Now I'm not a prophet of doom – not really – but I must admit I was beginning to think that the Department of Moans and Groans had got it right. People were going around complaining – even more than your lot do about the weather – and it was really an uphill struggle for a poor prophet trying to talk about hope.

After a while, I got a bit fed up, too. And it was then that God gave me this dream – sorry, vision. I seemed to be in a deep valley. There must have been a terrible battle there, sometime, I thought, because the whole valley was covered in skeletons. Honestly! And they weren't just lying there neatly the way they do in the movies. No, they were scattered all over the place. There were skulls lying next to shin bones, and jawbones next to toe bones – and they were brilliant white. No-one had invented biological washing powders then, so I guessed it must have been the sun that had done it. They were bleached and – well, I can't find any other way of saying it – bone dry.

I was wondering how I could get out, fast – before my bones got added to all of those. I tell you everything was so dry that there weren't even any vultures around. They like their food dead – but not *that* dead. Anyway, while I was wondering, I heard this voice. 'Strange,' I thought, 'I wonder who that is. What sort of person would come to a place like this? You'd either have to be mad or be God!'

When I listened carefully, I heard what the voice was saying. 'Hey, you! Human being! Homo Sapiens, or whatever your name is.'

'Who, me?' I asked.

'I don't see anyone else here, do you?' the voice answered.

'Er – what can I do for you?'

'Not a lot,' said the voice. 'It's really what I can do for you. Tell me, do you think that these dry bones can live?'

Now what sort of a question was that? 'God knows!' I said.

'Yes, that's right, I do,' said the voice and I nearly jumped out of my skin – and that would have been particularly uncomfortable in the heat.

'Oh, I'm very sorry,' I said, 'I didn't recognise your voice.'

'No, a lot of people don't,' said God. 'Now

I'm going to show you something really special. All you have to do is say the words I dictate to you.'

Then God told me what to say. I tried to remember it as best I could but it was awfully long.[1] 'Now listen here, you dry bones,' I said. 'God's going to join you all together again. Now all you toe bones have got to join up with foot bones, and you ankle bones look snappy and get hooked onto the other side. That's good! Now where are all you shin bones? All right – tibs and fibs if you want to be technical – you've got to join on to the anklebones, and pick up a kneecap along the way. Right on! Now, I want thigh bones, and pelvis bones, and I want lots of itsy bitsy back bones, and you all join together in just the right order. Now, give me some rib bones, some shoulder bones, some rib-ticklin' funny bones and where have those arm bones got to? Now some finger bones and, what've I forgotten? Well, would you believe it – what about some skull bones, then? And if you promise not to chatter you can have your jawbones too.'

Well, that about did it. When all the rattling died down the valley was a lot tidier, but they were still just lying there. 'Come on, now,' I said. 'Let's have some muscles and some tendons, and for goodness' sake put some skin on – you look revolting.' And it all happened! I could hardly believe it! But they were just as dead as when I'd started. Not a breath of life in a single one of them.

'Well, don't just stand there,' said God. 'Talk to the wind – get a bit of breath into them.'

So I called out to the four winds, and d'you know I'd hardly opened my mouth when there was such a whoosh you've never heard before and suddenly all the bodies began to move.

- They *wiggled their fingers*
- they *shook their hands*
- they *turned their heads*

They looked around and started to stand up. There were thousands of living bodies there. I couldn't help thinking that there was still something missing, but that was the end of the vision.

'That's how it's going to be,' God said to me. 'Where you think there's no hope, I'm going to bring new life. People will be happy again, and they'll know that I love them, and they'll all live together and really enjoy life.'

I was just about to say something when God interrupted me.

'By the way,' he said. 'You forgot their clothes. Must I think of everything?'

Our Story

Show the assembly the musical instruments, simply lying on a table top. You could suggest sitting and waiting until the instruments 'come to life' on their own! Let the children demonstrate the instruments simply or, if it's practicable, play a short piece of music together. The point is, of course, that the instruments can only 'come to life' with a bit of help from outside. Just like us!

Prayers

We're Sad

Sometimes, God, we're like dead bones,
just lying around waiting
for someone else to do something!
Please help us to be full of life,
ready to do things or you.

We're Glad

Thank you, God, for life!
Thank you for making this wonderful world
and for giving us something to do in it.
Help us to work with you
to make the whole world more lively.

Let's Pray for People

We pray for people who think there is no hope:
people who are ill, or sad;
people who always seem to see
the worst in everything.
Please, God, teach us all
that however bad things seem
there is always hope.

Songs

God made the earth (WUW)
Morning has broken (CAP)
Give me oil in my lamp (CAP)
Desert rain (CAP)
He's got the whole world in his hands (CAP)

---

[1] If preferred, in place of the paragraph, a group of children could sing the 'Dry Bones' song (see page 176)

Live Connections
God's Story

Narrator Hello, there! My name's Ezekiel, but you can call me Zeek if you like. I'm going to tell you about a really amazing vision that I had. I was in a deep valley with bones scattered all over the place. I tell you everything was so dry that there weren't even any vultures around. They like their food dead – but not *that* dead. Anyway, while I was wondering, I heard this voice.

God Hey! Zeek!

Narrator Strange, I wonder who that is. What sort of person would come to a place like this? You'd either have to be mad or be God!

God Hey, you! Human being! Homo Sapiens, or whatever your name is.

Narrator Who, me?

God I don't see anyone else here, do you?

Narrator Er – what can I do for you?

God Not a lot. It's really what I can do for you. Tell me, do you think that these dry bones can live?

Narrator God knows!

God Yes, that's right, I do.

Narrator Oh, I'm very sorry. I didn't recognise your voice.

God No, a lot of people don't. Now I'm going to show you something really special. All you have to do is say the words I dictate to you.

Narrator Okay. *(Listens)* Yes . . . Mmmm . . . Sorry, I missed that bit. Look, are you sure that's what you want? Okay, okay – you're the boss.[1]

---

[1] If preferred, in place of the next paragraph, a group of children could sing the 'Dry Bones' song (see page 176)

Now listen here, you dry bones, God's going to join you all together again. Now all you toe bones have got to join up with foot bones, and you ankle bones look snappy and get hooked onto the other side. That's good! Now where are all you shin bones? All right – tibs and fibs if you want to be technical – you've got to join on to the anklebones, and pick up a kneecap along the way. Right on! Now, I want thigh bones, and pelvis bones, and I want lots of itsy bitsy back bones, and you all join together in just the right order. Now, give me some rib bones, some shoulder bones, some rib-ticklin' funny bones and where have those arm bones got to? Now some finger bones and, what've I forgotten.? Well, would you believe it – what about some skull bones, then? And if you promise not to chatter you can have your jawbones too.

Now, what was the next bit again? *(Listens)*

Oh, yes – that's it. Let's have some muscles and some tendons, and for goodness' sake put some skin on – you look revolting.

Well, that's better – but they're not very lively are they?

God   Well, don't just stand there! Talk to the wind.

Narrator   So I called out to the four winds, and d'you know I'd hardly opened my mouth when there was such a whoosh you've never heard before and suddenly all the bodies started to move.

- They *wiggled their fingers*
- they *shook their hands*
- they *turned their heads*

I couldn't help thinking that there was still something missing, but that was the end of the vision.

God   That's how it's going to be. Where you think there's no hope, I'm going to bring new life. People will be happy again, and they'll know that I love them, and they'll all live together and really enjoy life. By the way, you forgot their clothes. Must I think of everything?

Trials and Temptations

Based on Matthew 4:1-11

BEFORE THE DAY

Get the children to collect (or draw their own) pictures of sports stars, circus performers, stunt men and women, etc. Then ask them to draw pictures or bring in photographs of people who care for them – parents, grandparents, brothers and sisters, neighbours etc. Pin or stick them on boards for display.

• Think about the actions for all the children to join in during the story.

ON THE DAY

Introduction

This morning, we'll be hearing about how Jesus was tempted to misuse his power. First, we're going to say our 'Thank you' prayer.

'Thank you' Prayer

Thank you, God, for all you give us,
thank you for the earth and sea;
thank you, God, for special people,
thank you, God, for making me.

God's Story

Jesus was sure God had a very special job for him; he'd always believed that, right from being a child, but it wasn't clear exactly what he should do.

'I think I'll get away for a bit and think,' he said to his mother. 'I really need to do a lot of praying, and work things out.'

'How long will you be?' asked Mary.

'Can't say,' said Jesus. 'God always seems to do things at his own speed, so don't wait up for me.'

I hope she didn't – because Jesus was away for well over a month. He found a really quiet place where he knew people didn't often go, and he spent the time praying and thinking, trying to hear what God was asking him to do.

One day, he heard a voice. Jesus knew it wasn't God; it had a cunning, deceitful sort of sound to it. You know the sort of voice – the kind people sometimes use when they're trying to get you to do something wrong. 'I bet you're hungry,' it said. 'Why don't you have something to eat?'

'Because I'm trying to concentrate,' answered Jesus. 'Anyway, there isn't anything.'

'Oh, come on! You know better than that!' said the voice. 'You know you're special to God. You could do anything you liked. So why not make some bread out of these stones? Might I recommend a nice granary wholemeal? What about a tasty fig and honey sandwich?'

'Oh no,' said Jesus, 'I'm not falling for that. Whatever power I have isn't for my benefit. It's got to be used to help others.'

'Oh, don't be so prissy!' said the voice. 'What's wrong with indulging yourself a little?'

'That's not what I'm here for,' said Jesus. 'Anyway, there are more important things than bread. The Bible says that we don't only live by bread, but by the word of God.'

'Oh, well,' said the voice, 'if you're going to start quoting the bible . . .' Then it went on. 'Look, if you've got a special mission, you've got to get people to listen to you. How are you going to do that?'

'That,' said Jesus, 'is exactly what I'm trying to work out. So why don't you just run away and play, and let me get on with it?'

'All right, then,' the voice continued, 'since you're good at quoting the bible, let me quote it to you. Doesn't it say somewhere that God won't let you come to harm? Why don't you go to the temple and jump off the tower? The bible says that God will send angels to catch you, and stop you hurting yourself. Now that would be a gimmick! You start walking back, and I'll go ahead and drum up the crowds.'

'I'm not here to do stunts,' said Jesus.

'Not stunts,' said the voice, 'miracles.'

'Stunts,' said Jesus. 'Miracles are only done to help people. Stunts are to show off and get attention. And since you want to throw bible texts around, you probably know that it says we shouldn't try to test God out.'

'Oh, that!' said the voice. 'It all depends what you mean by "test", doesn't it? Anyway, you should listen to me. I can be good for you. Why not take a look around?'

Jesus looked around and could hardly believe his eyes!

- He *looked to the left*
- he *looked to the right*
- and he *blinked in amazement!*

Was it a dream, or a vision, or was he imagining it? He seemed to be able to see all the wonderful things in the world: tall buildings and towers, with roofs shaped like onions but brightly coloured; huge triangular buildings that looked like synthetic mountains; wonderful forests and jungles with beautiful wild animals and birds; great mountain ranges covered in snow. It was like being up in a space shuttle with a telescope – except no one had thought of telescopes in those days.

'There!' said the voice. 'I can give it all to you. You could control everything. All you have to do is just do things my way. And while you're about it, you could put in a good word for us devils – we're having a hard time at present. So – do we have a deal?'

'What?' said Jesus. 'All that doesn't belong to you. You didn't make it. I'm sticking with God. He's the one who made all of that, and it belongs to him. So why don't you just go and find a quiet hole to crawl into?'

There was a long silence, and then a very shocked, faltering voice said, 'Are you sure you wouldn't like a sandwich? Call it a free sample. No obligation.'

'No!' said Jesus. 'Go on, push off!'

'Oh, all right,' said the voice, sulkily. 'But I didn't say I wouldn't come back. See you around.'

As Jesus set off for home, he knew things weren't going to be easy. The easy way would have been to do the things the voice had suggested. He'd chosen the harder way. He knew it would be difficult. He also knew that that horrible little voice would be back, but he wasn't too worried about it. After all, he'd turned down its best offer once, and he could do it again.

Our Story

Look at the two groups of pictures. Which, on the face of it, are the most spectacular – the most likely to pull a crowd? Then explain who the 'caring' group of pictures are, and what they do – or let the children themselves explain. So who's important now? Who would the children go to if they had hurt themselves, or were upset? Jesus never indulged in stunts or tricks: he cared.

Prayers

We're Sad

Please forgive us, God,
for worrying about ourselves
when we should be listening to you;
for showing off to get attention;
for trying to find the easy way
instead of the right way.
Please help us to trust you more.

We're Glad

Thank you, God, for always being with us,
even when life seems like a desert.
Thank you for helping us to do what's right,
even when other things seem more tempting.
Thank you, God, for just being you.

Let's Pray for People

We pray for people who have hard decisions
　to make;
politicians, torn between doing what is right
and trying to make themselves more popular;
people in business who want to be fair
to their customers and their workers;
teachers and others who have to be kind
but also have to be strict, sometimes.
Please God, help us all to make good decisions.

Songs

Out to the great wide world we go! (WUW)
It's me, O Lord (A)
Somebody greater (CAP)
Give me oil in my lamp (CAP)
Kum ba yah (CAP)

Trials and Temptations
God's Story

Narrator	Jesus was sure God had a very special job for him, but wasn't clear exactly what he should do.
Jesus	I think I'll get away somewhere quiet for a bit, Mother.
Mary	How long will you be gone?
Jesus	You never know with God – don't wait up.
Narrator	Jesus stayed away for well over a month. One day, he heard a cunning, deceitful little voice.
Devil	I bet you're hungry. Why not have something to eat?
Jesus	I'm trying to concentrate. Anyway, there isn't anything.
Devil	Oh, come on! You know better than that! Why not make bread out of these stones? Might I recommend a nice fig sandwich?
Jesus	That's not what I'm here for. The bible says that we don't only live by bread, but by the word of God.
Devil	Oh, if you're going to quote the bible . . .Look, you've got to get people's attention. How will you do that?
Jesus	That is exactly what I'm trying to work out. So why not just run away and play, and let me get on with it?
Devil	Well, since you're good at quoting the bible, doesn't it say that God won't let you get hurt? Why not jump off the temple tower? Now there's a gimmick!
Jesus	I'm not here to do stunts.
Devil	*(Persuasively)* Not stunts: Miracles!
Jesus	Stunts. Miracles are to help people. Stunts are to show off. And Scripture says we shouldn't test God out.

Devil	Oh, that! It all depends what you mean by 'test', doesn't it? Anyway, you should listen to me. I can be good for you. Why don't you take a look around?
Jesus	I don't need to. The answer's not out there; it's in me.
Devil	Oh, don't be such a stuffed toga! Live a little! Dream a little!
Narrator	Jesus looked around and could hardly believe his eyes! • He *looked to the left* • he *looked to the right* • and he *blinked in amazement* He could see all the wonderful things in the world: tall buildings and towers, with onion-shaped roofs; huge triangular buildings like synthetic mountains; wonderful jungles with beautiful wild animals and birds; it was like being up in a space shuttle with a telescope – except no one had invented telescopes in those days.
Devil	I can give it all to you if you just do things my way. And while you're about it, you could put in a good word for us devils; we're having a hard time at present. Do we have a deal?
Jesus	All that isn't yours to give. I'm sticking with God, so why don't you just find a quiet hole to crawl into?
Narrator	There was a long silence, and when the voice came again, it sounded different.
Devil	*(Weakly)* Are you sure you wouldn't like a sandwich? Call it a free sample. No obligation.
Jesus	I've already said no! So go on, push off!
Devil	*(Sulkily)* All right, but I'll be back. See you around.
Narrator	As Jesus set off for home, he knew he'd chosen the harder way. He also knew that that horrible little voice would be back, but he wasn't too worried about it. After all, he'd turned down its best offer once, and he could do it again.

Jesus makes Matthew Rich

Based on Matthew 9:9-13

BEFORE THE DAY

Get the children to collect containers and place the 'wrong' things inside them: a hat in a shoebox, for example, or sugar in a coffee jar. You could put a different dust jacket on a book. Just for a surprising twist, you might like to put the right things in one or two of them.

• Think about the actions for all the children to join in during the story.

ON THE DAY

Introduction

Our story this morning is about someone who was changed by meeting Jesus. First, we're going to say our 'Thank you' prayer.

'Thank you' Prayer

Thank you, God, for all you give us,
thank you for the earth and sea;
thank you, God, for special people,
thank you, God, for making me.

God's Story

When the Romans invaded Israel, most of the Israelites were very angry about it, but not everyone. Matthew knew that wherever there are soldiers there are money. One day the local Roman governor sent for him and said, 'How would you like to collect taxes for me?'

'That depends,' Matthew answered. 'What's in it for me?'

'Whatever you like,' answered the Governor. 'I don't care how much you cheat these people, just as long as you get the taxes in.'

'I'm not sure,' said Matthew.

'Well, let me help you make up your mind,' said the Governor – with a smile that was just a little too nice. 'If you work for me, I'll let you keep your head.'

'Yes, yes, of course, Your Excellency!' Matthew babbled in panic. 'It would be an honour to work for the glorious Roman Empire.'

So, next morning, Matthew was in a new office with a big desk and chair, and with a notice on the outside saying *All Taxes Collected. No credit – No I.O.U.s – No Forged Fivers, Dubious Dollars or Duff Denarii.*

Matthew quickly became very rich, but he found that there was a price to his wealth. When he met his old friend Adam in the street, Adam didn't say hello. 'Hey,' shouted Matthew, 'You blind or something?'

'Not so blind I can't recognise a traitor when I see one!' answered Adam, and kept on walking. When Matthew went home after work he found dreadful words written on his front door: like 'Traitor' and 'Filthy Scum'. He had to have armed guards with him the whole time – he couldn't even pop down the road to buy a pomegranate without three big men to keep him company. He began to wonder whether being so rich was worth it.

One day, he was sitting at his desk having an argument with a taxpayer. 'You're charging too much,' the man was saying.

'Look, Smartie-pants,' said Matthew sarcastically, 'If you had to do this rotten job you'd charge a lot, too.'

'Oh, hearts and flowers!' replied the other man. 'Some people would be glad to have a job at all, with the way things are going. Ever since this lot took over, *decent* people haven't been able to make an honest living.'

Then a new voice joined in. 'You having a spot of bother, Matthew?'

Matthew looked up and saw Jesus standing there. Jesus always said there were more important things than money, and Matthew used to think that was silly, but not any more – and only partly because he hadn't got any friends to say it to. If the truth be told, he was beginning to think the chap had a point. Suddenly, he sat up bolt upright in his chair.

'Tell you what,' he said to his client, 'Why don't we just forget the whole thing?'

'What?' said the man, in amazement.

'Go away,' said Matthew. 'Keep your money. I don't know what you see in the lousy stuff any way! Here you are, everybody.'

- He *handed out money*
- then he started *throwing it around*
- then he *washed his hands*

Matthew turned to Jesus. 'That's it!' he said. 'I've had it with money.'

'Don't blame the money,' said Jesus. 'We all need a bit of that. Your problem is that you're addicted to it – and that's what's wrong. Now if you were with me, you'd never have the chance to get addicted to anything – there's never enough of it around!'

Matthew looked at Jesus, and the friends he had around him, with their creased clothes and untidy hair. 'If you don't mind my saying so,' he said, 'you're not exactly an advert for simple living, are you?'

'Oh, I don't know,' said Jesus. 'No-one writes nasty things on my front door, because I haven't got one – and I don't have trouble with my tailor, either. I'll tell you what I have got, though. I've got friends. If I fancy a nice comfortable bed for the night, there's always somewhere I can go. And when it comes to money . . .'

'All right! said Matthew. 'You can start by coming for lunch with me. I've had it with this lousy job!'

When the religious leaders saw where Jesus was going, they were horrified. 'Jesus mixes with the wrong people!' they said.

'Well, if you're as good as you think you are, Jesus answered, 'you don't need me anyway. Doctors don't do house calls for people who are fit.'

As soon as the meal was over, Matthew told his bodyguard, 'I'm resigning. Tell the governor to find someone else.'

'He'll have your head for that!' grumbled the bodyguard.

'Ah,' said Matthew. 'He'll have to find me first, and as of right now I haven't got an address.'

Our Story

Ask the children to try to guess what's in the boxes. You could make it more fun by dividing them into teams and giving them options from which to choose the correct answer. You can make the point that things – and people – cannot always be judged by outward appearances.

Prayers

We're Sad

We're sorry, God, for times when we hurt people
because we think they're bad and we're good.
Teach us never to judge people,
always to remember that things may be
less simple, or obvious, than we think.

We're Glad

Thank you, God,
for forgiving us when we're not as good
as you would like us to be.
Thank you for those wonderful people
who always seem able to be nice to us
even when we don't deserve it.
Help us to be more like them.

Let's Pray for People

We pray for people who think they are good,
and people who think they are bad;
people who judge others,
and people who don't like themselves.
Help them to know your love,
which makes us all truly rich.

Songs

Jesus can make us truly rich (SS)
Jesus had all kinds of friends (WUW)
Out to the great wide world we go! (WUW)
Magic penny (A)
It's me, O Lord (A)
Give me oil in my lamp (CAP)

Jesus makes Matthew Rich
God's Story

Narrator When the Romans invaded Israel, most of the Israelites were very angry about it – but not Matthew. He could make a profit out of anything – including an invasion. One day the Roman governor sent for him.

Governor How would you like to collect taxes for me?'

Matthew That depends. What's in it for me?

Governor Whatever you like. I don't care how much you cheat these people, just as long as you get the taxes in.

Matthew Sounds good, but I'm not sure. Everyone will hate me.

Governor Yes, but if you refuse me I might hate you.

Matthew Yes, yes, of course, Your Excellency! It would be an honour to work for the glorious Roman Empire.

Narrator So, next morning, Matthew was in a new office with a big desk and chair, and with a notice on the outside saying *All Taxes Collected. No credit – No I.O.U.s – No Forged Fivers or Duff Denarii.* Matthew quickly became very rich – but unhappy.

Matthew It's awful! I haven't any friends any more. People call me names, and write things on my front door, and I can't even pop down the road to buy a pomegranate without a bodyguard.

Narrator One day, he was having an argument with a taxpayer.

Taxpayer You're charging too much.

Matthew Look, Smartie-pants, if you had to do this rotten job . . .

Taxpayer Oh, hearts and flowers! Some people would be glad to have a job at all.

Jesus You having a spot of bother, Matthew?

Narrator	Matthew looked up and saw Jesus. He'd always thought Jesus was a useless, woolly minded romantic – saying silly things like there were more important things than money. Suddenly, he sat bolt upright.
Matthew	Tell you what, let's just forget the whole thing. Go away. Keep your money. I don't know what you see in the lousy stuff any way! Nothing but trouble, if you ask me. Here you are, everybody. • He *handed out money* • then he started *throwing it around* • then he *washed his hands* That's it, Jesus! I've had it with money. Filthy stuff
Jesus	Don't blame the money – we all need a bit of that. Your problem is that you're addicted to it. Now if you were with me, you'd never have the chance to get addicted to anything – there's never enough of it around!
Matthew	If you don't mind my saying so, your appearance isn't exactly an advert for simple living, is it?
Jesus	Oh, I don't know. No-one writes nasty things on my front door, because I haven't got one – and I don't have trouble with my tailor, either. I'll tell you what I have got, though. I've got friends – I'm never short of a place to stay – and when it comes to money . . .
Matthew	All right! You can start by coming for lunch with me.
Narrator	The religious leaders were horrified – and said so.
Pharisee	That Jesus fellow mixes with all the wrong people!
Jesus	Well, if you're as good as you think you are, you don't need me. Doctors don't do house calls for people who are fit. By the way, Matthew, you do realise that if you resign the Governor will have your head for it?
Matthew	He'll have to find me first, and as of right now I haven't got an address.

Don't be Stingy

Based on Matthew 13:1-9

BEFORE THE DAY

Collect some empty packets from seeds which use different kinds of soil – acid, alkaline, sheltered, sunny etc. Put the packets onto a board and label each one, e.g: 'I like rich soil'.

• Think about the actions for all the children to join in during the story.

ON THE DAY

Introduction

We're having a bit of a gardening session today! First, we're going to say our 'Thank you' prayer.

'Thank you' Prayer

Thank you, God, for all you give us,
thank you for the earth and sea;
thank you, God, for special people,
thank you, God, for making me.

God's Story

Jesus wanted to show how generous God is with his love. So he told a story a bit like this one.

Sally was a farmer. She grew quite a lot of different crops, and she always had enough to feed her family and plenty to sell so that they could have some money to buy the things they couldn't grow. Everyone knew what a good farmer Sally was; everyone that is except her next door neighbour, Jake.

Jake didn't like waste. He hated seeing anything, no matter how small, not being used as well as possible. Now that's not such a bad thing, up to a point – sensible people don't waste valuable things – but Jake took it to ridiculous extremes. He would lean over the fence, while Sally was working hard in her garden, and say things like, 'You've got to make as much profit as you can, you know,' or, 'You ought to target your resources where they will be most effective.' Sally didn't really understand what all that meant, but she enjoyed her work and it always seemed to provide for her. She liked Jake, as well, even though he was a pain in the posterior most of the time; so she didn't say hurtful things back, but just smiled and nodded – and ignored him!

Sally's crops were doing very well, and one day she said to her husband, Tom, 'I think we should grow our own wheat. It's silly to go and buy flour when we could produce our own.'

So Sally found a nice little plot of land, and got it ready for sowing. Jake looked over the fence. 'Growing some wheat, are we?' he said. 'No money in wheat, these days, the big boys have got all that buttoned up. You'll never grow enough to make it pay. What d'you pay for your seeds? More than you should, I'll bet. You've got to keep your unit costs in mind, you know.'

Sally smiled. After she had got the ground ready she went into the potting shed and got her precious bag of seeds. She went out and started scattering them around. Poor Jake nearly had a heart attack!

- He *leaned on the fence*
- and he *shook his head*
- and he *stroked his beard*

'You can't just go scattering seeds around like that,' he said. 'Target your resources – how often must I tell you! Look, you've gone and spilt some among those thistles. You'd better get them out – they'll never grow there.'

'Thank you,' said Sally, and carried on sowing her seed. Then Jake got really agitated, and said, 'Hey! Mind the path! Nothing will grow there, you know.'

'No, said Sally, calmly, 'I don't suppose it will.'

'Mind the rockery!' roared Jake. 'Really, Sally, I don't know how you expect ever to make a living as a farmer! Just like a woman!'

Sally decided to ignore that. She finished off her work, wished Jake a good afternoon and went inside. Jake just stood there, leaning on the fence, and shaking his head in despair.

Sally looked and saw a flock of birds on the path, eating the seeds she had dropped there. 'Well,' she thought, 'They've got to eat as well. And if they eat the seed on the path, they're leaving the rest alone.'

A few days later, Tom got really excited. 'Your seeds are growing,' he said to Sally. Sure enough, the rockery was sprouting wheat. 'I wouldn't get too excited,' she said to Tom. 'There's not enough soil there, so it won't last.' When the sun got really hot, the wheat was scorched and it died. 'Not to worry,' said Sally, 'I expected that.'

Next time Sally was outside, Jake was leaning on the fence as usual. 'I told you not to do it,' he said. 'It won't grow, you know.' Then he looked over to the thistle patch. 'There's a bit sprouting there,' he said, 'but it won't last. You mark my words.'

He was right. The thistles were very strong weeds, and they'd had a lot of time to get well set in. So they just choked the new wheat shoots, and never gave them a chance.

'See,' said Jake. 'You women should really listen to us men. I don't know why your husband doesn't keep you straight.'

Sally laughed, 'Tom wouldn't know a cauliflower from a buttercup! He's a fisherman!' And she chuckled as she went inside. Tom laughed when she told him, too.

Over the next few months, the plot of land started to change. Little green shoots appeared first, and Sally and Tom started to get excited. Then the shoots grew tall, and very soon they were dense and high enough for rabbits and field mice to hide in them without being seen. Sally and Tom watched as the colour changed gradually, and eventually they had a wonderful plot of land filled with golden wheat waving gently in the wind.

As soon as it was ripe, Sally got Tom to act as labourer for her and they harvested the wheat. Jake looked over the fence and gave them occasional advice. 'Don't miss any,' he said. 'You've got to exploit the potential of your investment to the full.'

When the wheat was gathered in, they weighed it and Sally was overjoyed. 'According to what I've worked out,' she said to Tom, 'those seeds we bought have given us thousands more in return. Some of them must have produced thirty, or sixty or even a hundred times as much!'

'Hmmph!' snorted Jake over the fence. 'If you'd been more careful, you'd have had even more.'

'If I'd followed your advice,' retorted Sally, 'I'd never have sown any seeds at all.'

Our Story

Draw attention to the board. Whatever kind of soil we find, God has provided something that will grow in it. It really is true that God loves *everything* that he has made!

Prayers

We're Sad

Please forgive us, God, for being so careful –
with our money, with our things,
and most of all with our love.
Teach us how much joy we can get
from throwing love around!

We're Glad

Thank you, God!
You don't take advice from 'wise' people;
you scatter love around
as though it's going out of fashion!
Thank you for giving us so much.

Let's Pray for People

Let's pray especially for lonely people.
Some people are lonely because
other people are too 'careful' with their love.
Others are lonely because they themselves
are too selfish, afraid of losing out.
Please, God, help us all to understand
that you never run out of love,
and however much we 'waste'
you will always give us more.

Songs

God is making a wonderful world (WUW)
We can plough and dig the land (WUW)
Out to the great wide world we go! (WUW)
Sing a song of weather (WW)
Magic penny (A)
Love is his word (A)
Think of a world without any flowers (CAP)
When I needed a neighbour (CAP)

Don't be Stingy!
God's Story

Narrator Jesus wanted to show how generous God is with his love. So he told a story a bit like this one:

It's about Sally, who was a very good farmer – but her neighbour, Jake, didn't approve of her. He would lean on the fence while Sally worked, and make comments.

Jake You've got to make as much profit as you can, you know. You ought to target your resources.

Narrator One day, Sally decided to start growing her own wheat, to make bread. She started getting the land ready for sowing, while Jake looked over the fence.

Jake Growing some wheat? No money in it these days; the big boys have got it buttoned up. You'll never make it pay. What d'you pay for your seeds? Too much, I'll bet. You've got to keep unit costs in mind, you know.

Narrator When Sally sowed her seeds, Jake was shocked.

- He *leaned on the fence*
- and he *shook his head*
- and he *stroked his beard*

Jake You can't just go scattering seeds around like that! Target your resources – how often must I tell you! Look, you've gone and spilt some among those thistles. Hey! Mind the path! Nothing will grow there.

Sally No, I don't suppose it will.

Jake Mind the rockery! Really, Sally, you'll never make a proper living as a farmer! Just like a woman!

Narrator Sally decided to ignore that. She finished off her work and went inside. Jake just stood there, leaning on the fence, and shaking his head in despair. Sally looked out of the window and saw a flock of birds on the path, eating the seeds she had dropped there.

Sally	Well, they've got to eat as well. And if they eat the seed on the path, they're leaving the rest alone.
Narrator	Very soon, wheat started to sprout – in the rockery.
Sally	I won't get too excited. There's not enough soil there, so it won't last. Still, I expected that.
Narrator	Sure enough, when the sun got really hot, the wheat was scorched and it died.
Jake	I said it wouldn't grow. There's a bit sprouting there, in the thistles, but it won't last. You mark my words.
Narrator	He was right. The thistles were very strong and they just choked the new wheat shoots.
Jake	See? You women should really listen to us men. I don't know why your husband doesn't sort you out.
Sally	What, Tom? Tom wouldn't know a cauliflower from a buttercup! He's a fisherman. Oh, what a joke – Tom will love that one!
Narrator	Over the next few months, little green shots appeared and grew tall. Very soon they were dense and high enough for rabbits and field mice to hide in them. Sally and Tom watched as the colour changed gradually, and eventually they had a wonderful crop of golden wheat waving gently in the wind. As soon as it was ripe, Sally and Tom harvested the corn, while Jake looked over the fence and gave them advice.
Jake	Don't miss any. Make the most of your investment.
Narrator	When the wheat was gathered in, Sally was overjoyed.
Sally	Some of those seeds must have produced thirty, or sixty or even a hundred times as much!
Jake	If you'd been more careful, you'd have had even more.
Sally	If I'd followed your advice, I'd never have sown any seeds at all.

The Barley and the Bindweed

Based on Matthew 13:24-30

BEFORE THE DAY

Get the children to paint pictures of flowers, shrubs, vegetables etc. on pieces of paper, and write 'You are a . . .' on each one. When they are dry, fold them and put them all in a container ready for the assembly.

• Think about the actions for all the children to join in during the story.

ON THE DAY

Introduction

We're going to play a kind of gardening game in a little while, but first, we'll say our 'Thank you' prayer.

'Thank you' Prayer

Thank you, God, for all you give us,
thank you for the earth and sea;
thank you, God, for special people,
thank you, God, for making me.

God's Story

Sally and Jake were both farmers, but they farmed in very different ways. Jake was greedy. He always farmed every bit of his land, and never left anything behind when he harvested.

Sally was a lot more relaxed about things. She used to leave a bit of one of her fields wild to encourage butterflies and other beautiful wildlife. Jake thought she was mad.

'You'll never make any money out of butterflies,' he used to say. 'You have to get everything you can out of your land – that's what good farming's about.'

Sally told her workers to vary the crops so that the fields had a change, and to leave one field each year without anything growing in it. 'We've got to take care of the land,' she used to say. 'Then it will take care of us.'

Jake thought this was just a load of sentimental nonsense. 'It's a matter of good stewardship,' he used to say. 'You've got to get all you can from the land.'

'No,' said Sally. 'Good stewardship is about caring for the land – and it'll give you more in the long run.'

'Bah! Humbug!' Exclaimed Jake, and waited for Sally to get really poor. 'When she is, I can buy her fields cheaply,' he thought.

Well, Jake watched and waited, and every harvest he thought he'd see Sally packing it in because it wasn't paying. But what he actually saw was Sally's farm doing better and better.

- She *dug*
- she *hoed*
- and she *watered the crops*

After a little while, Jake's farm started to produce smaller crops. 'I can't understand it,' his foreman said one day. 'The cabbages always used to do well in that field, but they're just not growing now.'

'Well,' said Jake, 'we'll just have to put more seed in to compensate.'

Sally overheard the conversation. 'If you don't mind my saying so,' she said, 'that'll just make it worse. You're taking all the goodness out of the land. Why not give it a rest for a year, and grow something different?'

'I do mind you saying so, actually,' he snapped. 'Mind your own business!'

Jake was really jealous of Sally. 'She doesn't work half as hard as I do,' he complained to his labourer. 'And just look at her crops!'

Well, the years went by and Jake just could not understand what was happening. Sally's farm was thriving, with lovely rich soil producing good crops while Jake' crops got smaller and smaller. Then his soil began to go all powdery and dry, and every time there was a strong wind some of it blew away and landed on Sally's farm.

'That's the problem!' thought Jake. 'She's got better soil than mine. Now if I had her soil I could grow ten times as much as she does, but I can't afford to buy her land from her even if she would sell. If only I could find some way of reducing the value of her farm.' Then he had a terrible idea.

Although he couldn't grow good food crops any more, Jake had plenty of thistles and dandelions, and enormous quantities of bindweed. So he dug up some of them, and put them into his greenhouse where he tended them very carefully.

Jake saved all the seeds the weeds produced, and then late at night, while Sally was fast asleep in bed, he went out and headed for Sally's best fields. And there, among the crops, he scattered the thistle, dandelion and bindweed seeds. Then he sneaked home and waited.

One morning, Sally's foreman came running up and said, 'Quick! Come and look at the fields!' Sally hurried off to see what all the fuss was about, and there, all mixed in among the crops were thousands of nasty looking weeds.

'I can't think what went wrong,' stammered the foreman apologetically.

'Don't worry, it's not your fault,' Sally assured him. 'someone's been up to mischief, and I think I know who.'

'Well, I'd better get them out,' said the foreman.

'Oh no! Don't do that!' exclaimed Sally. 'You'll probably pull up some good plants as well. No, just let them grow together. My crops are good enough to stand a bit of competition from a few weeds. We can separate them at harvest.'

Sally was quite right: her crop stood up to the weeds very well, and when the harvest time came they had a grand sort out.

Jake's little plan hadn't worked at all. In fact, it was he who went out of business, because he'd destroyed the very land upon which he depended. Then Sally bought his farm at a bargain price and set about correcting the harm that Jake had done.

Our Story

Hand out the different pieces of folded paper to children at random, around the group. Then ask them to open them and say what they've got. If the children really were flowers or vegetables, of course, you probably wouldn't have all those things growing in the same field, but that's the nice thing about being a human being – we can all grow up together, whatever we are!

Prayers

We're Sad

Dear God, we're sorry for our jealousy.
Help us to be truly happy
when other people succeed,
and to be ready to learn from them.

We're Glad

Thank you, God, for talented people.
Thank you for people who succeed
at discovering new things,
at healing people who are sick,
at creating beautiful art.
Thank you for the pleasure they give us.

Let's Pray for People

Let's Pray for People
Some people are unhappy
because they don't feel 'successful'.
But it's not compulsory to be brilliant, is it?
Please God, help them to enjoy being truly
   human,
and to be proud of that.
Teach us to value people for what they are,
not for what they do,
and give us grace to show it.

Songs

God made the earth (WUW)
We can plough and dig the land (WUW)
Sing a song of weather! (WW)
Thank you, O God, for all our friends (WW)
All things bright and beautiful (CAP)
Somebody greater (CAP)
God knows me (CAP)

The Barley and the Bindweed
God's Story

Narrator   Sally and Jake were both farmers, and they had been friends once, although they farmed in very different ways. Jake was greedy. He grew as much as he possibly could and sold it for the very highest possible price. Every single square inch of Jake's farm was always growing something. Sally used to leave a bit of her land wild to encourage butterflies and other wildlife.

Jake   You'll never make any money out of butterflies.

Sally   We've got to take care of the land, and not ask too much of it. Then it will take care of us.

Jake   Sentimental nonsense! It's a matter of good stewardship. You've got to get all you can from the land.

Sally   No, good stewardship is about caring for the land – and it'll give you more in the long run.

Jake   Bah! Humbug! *(Aside to audience)* when she gets really poor I'll buy her fields at a knockdown price. Then I'll show her how a *real* farmer works the land!

Narrator   Sally worked very hard on her farm.

- She *dug*
- She *hoed*
- and she *watered the crops*

Narrator   Sally's farm did better and better, while Jake's crops got smaller. His foreman was worried.

Foreman 1   I can't understand it. The cabbages always used to do well in that field, but for the last year or two they've definitely been smaller.'

Jake   All the crops get smaller every year. Well, we'll just have to put more seed in to compensate.

Narrator	Sally overheard the conversation.
Sally	If you don't mind my saying so that'll just make it worse. You're taking all the goodness out of the land. Why not give it a rest for a year, and grow something different?
Jake	I do mind you saying so, actually. You go and mind your own business, Mrs. Knowitall!
Narrator	Jake was really jealous of Sally, and started to hatch a very nasty plan. Although he couldn't grow good food crops any more, Jake had plenty of weeds because they will grow anywhere, as any gardener will tell you. So he collected the seeds from them, and one night, while Sally was fast asleep in bed, he scattered the seeds among her crops. Very soon, Sally's foreman came running up to her, very upset.
Foreman 2	Quick! Come and look at the fields!
Narrator	Sally hurried off to see what all the fuss was about, and there, all mixed in among the crops, were thousands of nasty-looking weeds.
Foreman 2	I can't think what went wrong.
Sally	Don't worry, it's not your fault. I think I know who's done this.
Foreman 2	Well, I'd better get them out.
Sally	Oh no! Don't do that! You'll probably pull up some good plants as well. No, just let them grow together. My crops are good enough to stand a bit of competition from a few weeds. When we harvest it, that will be the time to separate them out.
Narrator	Sally was quite right: her crop stood up to the weeds very well, and at harvest time they had a grand sort out. Jake soon went out of business, because he'd destroyed the very land upon which it depended. Then Sally bought his farm at a bargain price and set about correcting the harm that Jake had done.

The Sale of the Century

Based on Matthew 13:45-46

BEFORE THE DAY

Get the children to think about the things that are most important to them. You may need to steer them away from computers and roller skates, perhaps by specifying 'people', 'sounds', 'smells' and so on. Let them write them down, or perhaps paint pictures. Finally, put them in a box and label it 'Class X's Treasure Box' in large letters.

• Think about the actions for all the children to join in during the story.

ON THE DAY

Introduction

In a little while, we shall be thinking about the things that are important to us. First, we're going to say our 'Thank you' prayer.

'Thank you' Prayer

Thank you, God, for all you give us,
thank you for the earth and sea;
thank you, God, for special people,
thank you, God, for making me.

God's Story

Abe was a very wealthy man. He had a big house, with lots of rooms, and each room was full of beautiful furniture. He was never cold at night, because he had lovely warm rugs on his bed, and thick carpets on his floors. At every window hung colourful, heavy curtains which kept out the draughts and looked impressive as well.

Every day, Abe fed on the best food money could buy, and drank excellent wines. He really knew how to enjoy life, and he could afford to do it. His friends used to say that even if the whole world went bankrupt, Abe would be all right. He was incredibly rich.

How had he got rich? Well, Abe was a merchant. That meant that he bought and sold things – but not just any old things. Abe was a pearl trader. He used to make long journeys to visit the pearl fishers. They would spend all day diving in the sea looking for oysters which had pearls in them, and then they would sell the pearls they found to people like Abe who would take them to the markets and sell them to people like you and me. It was a lovely business to be in, and Abe really enjoyed it.

And yet, Abe was not really happy. Even with his fine house, his large stables full of beautiful horses and camels, his wonderful gardens stretching as far as the eye could see – even with all that, he was not really happy. He was sure there was a beautiful pearl out there somewhere, which he had not yet seen. Abe didn't just trade pearls for money – he actually enjoyed pearls for themselves. And he had a lifelong ambition to find his perfect pearl, but he knew that he would probably never be lucky enough to fulfil it.

Then one day, it happened.

He was walking along the beach where the pearl fishers worked when he felt a nudge and heard a voice say, 'Hey, Guv, want to see something really special?'

There was something familiar about the voice, which made Abe turn and look. It was Josh, one of the pearl fishers. 'It's a pearl!' Josh said. 'That pearl you've always been after.'

'Look, Josh, I don't mind a joke,' said Abe, 'but it's been a really hard day, so just drop it will you?'

'No wind up, Guv – honest!' said Josh. 'Go on – won't hurt to look. What've you got to lose?'

'All right, Josh,' said Abe, wearily, 'but it'd better not be a wind-up. Let's have a look, then.'

Josh looked horrified. 'What, here? D'you want the whole world to know about it? Lord love me, Guv, I couldn't sleep safe in me bed if I thought anyone knew.' With that, Josh led Abe to a deserted corner of the beach, and then, looking furtively around him, drew back some branches from the mouth of a cave. 'No one knows about this, Guv,' he said. 'Get in, quick.'

Once inside, Josh lit a candle and rummaged under a pile of moss. Then, before Abe's amazed eyes, he brought out the most wonderful pearl Abe had ever seen. More than that, it was beyond anything he could ever have imagined. It was perfectly round, with a silky smooth surface, and seemed to absorb the light of the candle. In return, it gave off all the colours of the rainbow. Abe was absolutely entranced by it.

- He *held it up to the light*
- and *polished it on his sleeve*
- then he *held it up to the light* again

And in that moment he knew that this was the chance to fulfil his life's ambition.

As Abe turned to face Josh, he did his best to look casual. 'It's, er, quite a nice one,' he said. 'How much d'you want for it.'

Josh was now full of confidence. He'd known that all he had to do was to get Abe to look at it and it would be sold. 'Come off it, Guvnor,' he said. 'It's not "quite nice" – it's absolutely stupendous. You've never seen anything like it before and I doubt you will again. Now if you want it it's yours but if you don't I can soon find another punter.'

'Oh, no! Don't do that! gasped Abe. 'How much d'you want for it?'

'Well,' said Josh. 'I'm not a greedy man. All I want is a big house, a stable full of fine horses, and enough money to keep me in luxury the rest of my life. Shall we say a million?'

Abe nearly died of heart failure. That would take everything he'd got. His beautiful house, his stables, his fine clothes and furniture – everything he'd worked for all his life would have to be sold to buy this one pearl.

'I don't know,' he said. 'That's an awful lot of money.'

'It's an awful lot of pearl,' said Josh. 'Still, if you don't want it . . .'

'Hold on – I never said that!' said Abe, hastily. 'All right. I'll get the money.'

Abe sold his house, with all its furniture and equipment, and went to live in a tent. He sold his horses and camels, and all the other things he had. Then he went to the bank and drew out all his money, and eventually he just managed to scrape together the million that Josh wanted. Then he went back to see Josh. 'There you are,' he said. 'You can count it if you like.'

'I will,' said Josh, and when he had he handed over the pearl to Abe. 'Tell me, Abe,' he said, 'What makes you want this so badly that you've sold everything you worked for just to buy this one pearl?'

'Well,' said Abe. 'Some things are worth much more than money, or comfort. You have to be prepared to give up the less important things if you want to have what's really valuable.'

Our Story

Open the treasure box and take out the contents one by one. Either ask the children to describe their 'treasures' or, if they are a bit timid, explain for them. Then ask the rest of the assembly which they would treasure most.

Prayers

We're Sad

Please forgive us, God,
for clinging to things
which can't make us happy,
and ignoring the things that can.
Help us to treasure love and goodness,
and each other.

We're Glad

Thank you, God, for giving us your love.
Thank you for showing us
just how important we are
by sacrificing everything for us.
Teach us to love and value one another
the way you love and value us.

Let's Pray for People

We pray for people who miss out
on the really wonderful things of life,
because they're trying to cling on
to things that aren't as good.
Please, God, help all people
to share your sense of values.

Songs

Out to the great wide world we go! (WUW)
Magic penny (A)
Love is his word (A)
The best gift (CAP)

The Sale of the Century
God's Story

Narrator	Abe was a very wealthy man. He had a big house, and fed on the best food money could buy. He was incredibly rich. How had he got rich? Well, he was a pearl trader. He used to make long journeys to visit the pearl fishers. They would sell him the pearls they found and he would take them to the markets and sell them to people like you and me. It was a lovely business, and Abe enjoyed it – but he wasn't really happy.
Abe	I'm sure there's a really beautiful pearl out there somewhere, and I want it.
Narrator	Then one day, it happened.
Josh	Hey, Guv. Want to see a the pearl of your dreams?
Abe	I don't mind a joke, Josh, but it's been a really hard day
Josh	No wind up Guv, honest! Go on – won't hurt to look.
Abe	All right, but it'd better be good. Let's have a look.
Josh	What, here? D'you want the whole world to know about it? Lord love me, Guv, I couldn't sleep safe in me bed if I thought anyone knew.
Narrator	Josh led Abe to a deserted cove, and furtively drew back some branches from the mouth of a cave.
Josh	No one knows about this, Guv,' he said. 'Get in, quick.'
Narrator	Once inside, Josh lit a candle and rummaged under a pile of moss. Then, before Abe's amazed eyes, he brought out the most wonderful pearl Abe had ever seen. More than that, it was beyond anything he could ever have imagined. It was perfectly round, silky smooth, and seemed to turn the light of the candle into all the colours of the rainbow. Abe was entranced.

- He *held it up to the light*
- and *polished it on his sleeve*
- then he *held it up to the light* again

Abe It's, er, quite a nice one. How much d'you want for it.

Josh Come off it, Guv'nor. It's not 'quite nice' – it's absolutely stupendous. You've never seen anything like it before and I doubt you will again. Now if you want it it's yours but if you don't I can soon find another punter.

Abe Oh, no! Don't do that! How much d'you want for it?

Josh Well, I'm not a greedy man. All I want is a big house, some fine horses, and enough money to keep me in luxury the rest of my life. Shall we say a million?

Narrator Abe nearly died of heart failure. That would take everything he'd got. His beautiful house, his stables, his fine clothes and furniture – everything he'd worked for all his life would have to be sold to buy this one pearl.

Abe I don't know – that's an awful lot of money.

Josh It's an awful lot of pearl. Still, if you don't want it . . .

Abe Hold on – I never said that! O K I'll get the money.

Narrator Abe sold his house, with all its furniture and equipment, and went to live in a tent. He sold his horses and camels, and all the other things he had. Then he went to the bank and drew out all his money, and eventually he just managed to scrape together the million that Josh wanted.

Abe There you are – a million – just what you asked for.

Josh Tell me, Guv, how come you've sold everything you worked for just to buy this one pearl?

Abe Well, some things are worth much more than money, or comfort. You have to be prepared to give up the less important things if you want to have what's really valuable.

Jesus Gets Angry

Based on Matthew 21:12-14

BEFORE THE DAY

Perhaps it isn't always wrong to be angry. Some people get angry about unfairness; others when they see people being bullied, and so on. Discuss with the children the things that make them angry, and make a list on a flipchart.

• Think about the actions for all the children to join in during the story.

ON THE DAY

Introduction

Soon, we're going to hear a story about some people who made Jesus very angry. First, we're going to say our 'Thank you' prayer.

'Thank you' Prayer

Thank you, God, for all you give us,
thank you for the earth and sea;
thank you, God, for special people,
thank you, God, for making me.

God's Story

Dan, the money changer was setting up his stall as usual in the temple. Next to him, in his accustomed place, was Joe, a dove merchant. People who went to the temple needed doves because they were used in the worship, so it made sense for them to be sold there. And they needed special money to put in the offering, so Dan was there to change their ordinary money into special temple money. That all seems perfectly reasonable. But you know the old saying, 'It ain't what you do it's the way that you do it'?

'I like it here,' Dan was saying. 'Better than standing outside in the rain.'

'Yes,' said Joe. 'Mind you, I sometimes get a bit embarrassed about the space we take up. It makes it difficult for less able people to get in when these stalls are all over the place.'

'Who cares about them?' scoffed Dan. 'They've never got any money anyway.'

'That's true,' said Joe, 'and of course there's another advantage to being in here.'

'What's that?' asked Dan.'

'Simple,' said Joe. 'It's harder for the customers to compare our prices with the ordinary shops. And once they're in they don't feel like going back out anyway, so we can charge extra.'

'You're right,' said Dan. 'It's a pretty good swindle – and it's legal!'

'Just a minute,' said Joe. 'What's all that noise outside?'

They listened carefully. There seemed to be some kind of celebration going on. They could just about make out words like 'Hosanna!' but they couldn't understand what it was about. Then a man they thought they recognised strode into the temple and stood looking around in a disapproving way.

'Isn't that that Jesus character?' asked Joe. 'He doesn't look very happy – d'you think he's going to cause trouble?'

'What! Him?' laughed Dan. 'He's a wimp! Talks about "love" and "forgiveness" all the time. He actually tells people that if someone hits them they should let them do it again?'

'You're kidding!' exclaimed Joe, and they roared with laughter.

The traders ignored Jesus.

• Dan *counted his money*
• Joe *stroked on of his doves*
• while Jesus *looked from side to side*

Jesus turned to Andrew. 'Look at this!' he said. 'We had to climb over sick and disabled people to get in here, and all the space is taken up by these money-grabbing swindlers!'

Andrew was worried. 'Why don't we just go and find a quiet drink somewhere?' he asked. 'It's been a big day for you.'

Jesus didn't hear him. He was too concerned with what was happening.

'What do you people think you're doing?' he asked, just a little too quietly.

'Just a bit of honest trade, sir,' grinned Joe. 'Can I interest you in a pair of doves? Best prices in town.'

'Best for you, you mean,' said Jesus. And

then, without warning, he grabbed the front of Joe's stall and turned it over. The cages burst open and doves started flying everywhere. Then Jesus went over to Dan.

'Now look here,' Dan said hastily, 'I've got a licence to trade here; I paid a high bribe – I mean tax – for it.' But Jesus wasn't listening. He grabbed Dan's tray of money and threw it on the floor, and then picked up his table and turned it upside down. Well, there was pandemonium. Worshippers were scrabbling around in the dust and fighting over the most valuable coins. Then Jesus went over to the animal pens and drove the animals out of the temple. The owners went after them to try to catch them, and Joe and Dan also decided to cut their losses and leave at the same time. The scramble for money died down as the best coins were snapped up, and by the time the temple police arrived it was all over. Well, nothing changes, does it!

Then a wonderful thing happened. Into the temple came a procession of people who had never been in there before. Some of them had to be carried or helped by others; some were blind and had to have someone to guide them. They came over to where Jesus was standing, still a little out of breath, and the first one, who was leaning on a stick spoke to him.

'Thank you,' he said. 'We haven't been able to get in before. The traders took up so much room, and all the people bustling about doing their shopping meant that only the really fit people could cope with it.'

'I know,' said Jesus, 'and it makes me angry! But while you're here why don't we do something about that leg of yours?'

Jesus took hold of his hand and suddenly the man's leg grew strong again. Jesus moved on to the next person. Soon the temple was full of people laughing, singing and praising God while they jumped and ran around celebrating their new found health and strength.

From then on, a lot of new people joined in things at the temple, who had never been able to get in before. They were very happy about it, although Dan and Joe and their friends weren't. But then, you can't please everybody, can you – so why try?

Our Story

Use the flipchart list to talk about what makes the children angry, *and what can be done about it*, eg if someone is being bullied tell a teacher, etc.

Prayers

We're Sad

We say patience is a virtue,
but sometimes that's an excuse.
We're sorry, God, for being too tolerant
when other people are getting hurt.
Help us to know when it's right to be patient,
and when we should protest.

We're Glad

Thank you, loving God,
for people who protest against evil.
Thank you for using them
to make the world a better place for us all.

Let's Pray for People

We pray for people who are kept out,
who aren't able to protest for themselves
and get brushed aside.
Especially we pray for disabled people
in a world run by the able bodied.
Please God, help us to be angry for them,
and give us the courage to protest.

Songs

I'm black, I'm white, I'm short, I'm tall (WUW)
Jesus had all kinds of friends (WUW)
Thank you, O God, for all our friends (WW)
Put your hand in the hand (A)
When I needed a neighbour (CAP)
If I had a hammer (CAP)

Jesus Gets Angry
God's Story

Narrator	Dan, the money changer was setting up his stall as usual in the temple, next to Joe, a dove merchant.
Dan	I like it here, Joe – better than being out in the rain.
Joe	Yes. Mind you, our stalls make it difficult for less able people to get in.
Dan	Who cares about them? They've never got any money.
Joe	That's true, and of course in here it's harder for the customers to compare our prices with the ordinary shops.
Dan	That's right. It's a pretty good swindle – and it's legal!
Joe	Just a minute, – what's all that noise outside?
Narrator	They listened carefully. It seemed to be some kind of celebration. They could just about make out words like 'Hosanna!' Then Jesus strode into the temple with his friends, and stood looking around.
Joe	He doesn't look very happy – he might cause trouble.
Dan	What! Him? He's a wimp! Talks about 'love' and 'forgiveness' all the time. He's a nobody – ignore him
Narrator	So they did.

- Dan *counted his money*
- Joe stroked one of his doves
- while Jesus *looked from side to side*

Jesus	There are sick and disabled people outside who can't get in, and all the space is taken up by these money-grabbing swindlers!
Narrator	Jesus went over to Joe.
Jesus	What do you people think you're doing?

Joe	Just a bit of honest trade, sir. Best prices in town.
Jesus	Best prices for you, you mean.
Narrator	And then, without warning, Jesus grabbed Joe's stall and turned it over. The cages burst open and doves flew everywhere. Then Jesus went over to Dan.
Dan	Now look here, I've got a licence to trade here; I paid a high bribe – I mean tax – for it.
Narrator	Jesus wasn't listening. He threw Dan's tray of money on the floor and overturned his table. After that, he drove the animals and all the traders out of the temple. By the time the temple police arrived it was all over. Well, nothing changes, does it! Then a wonderful thing happened. Into the temple came a procession of people who had never been in there before. Some couldn't walk and had to be helped by friends; others were blind and had to be guided. They came over to where Jesus was standing, still a little out of breath, and a woman with a stick spoke to him.
Esther	Thank you. We haven't been able to get in before. The traders took up so much room, and all the people bustling about doing their shopping meant that only the really fit people could cope with it.
Jesus	I know, and it makes me angry! Now you're here why don't we do something about that leg of yours?
Esther	I've tried every doctor in the area, but it's incurable.
Narrator	Jesus took hold of her hand, and suddenly the woman's leg grew strong again. Jesus moved on to the next person, and soon the temple was full of people laughing, singing and praising God while they jumped and ran around celebrating their new found health and strength. From then on, a lot of new people joined in things at the temple, who had never been able to get in before. They were very happy about it, although Dan and Joe and their friends weren't. But then, you can't please everybody, can you – so why try?

Nancy's Nightmare

Based on Matthew 25:31-end

BEFORE THE DAY

Discuss with the children ways in which they can respond to people's needs: carrying shopping, visiting a lonely neighbour, sending a card, giving to charity etc. Let them use their imaginations and draw pictures of these examples, which can then be fixed to a board ready for the assembly, with the heading 'You Did It For Me' over the top.

Important note:

This version has been carefully adapted to avoid encouraging children to open the door to strangers. Teachers may wish to reinforce the point that this story is about a grown up, and children can live it out by being kind to people they *know*.

• Think about the actions for all the children to join in during the story.

ON THE DAY

Introduction

In a little while, we'll be thinking about ways we can show that we love God by being kind to people. First, though, we're going to say our 'Thank you' prayer.

'Thank you' Prayer

Thank you, God, for all you give us,
thank you for the earth and sea;
thank you, God, for special people,
thank you, God, for making me.

God's Story

It was just a night like any other when Nancy went to bed, but what she didn't know was that everything was going to change.

The first inkling of that came when she found herself in a strange place without knowing how she'd got there. Gradually it began to dawn on her. 'I've died,' she thought. 'So this must be heaven.' Nancy had always known she'd go to heaven, because she knew what a good person she was. She always went to church, never used a naughty word, and always kept her home beautifully clean and saved her money carefully. So you can see why Nancy was very confident that she'd go to heaven. And here she was! Then she heard a voice. 'Hi, Nance! What you doing here?'

Nancy was horrified; it was Sheila, her neighbour. Now Sheila hadn't been near a church in forty years, except to get married – and the less said about that the better! Apart from that, she used to use words Nancy wouldn't dream of saying, and her house was always untidy. Well it would be: she was never there to clean it – always gallivanting off to cook at the night shelter, or visit people in prison. Nancy didn't hold with that. 'People shouldn't get themselves in trouble in the first place,' was how she saw it. Well, Sheila wouldn't get into heaven!

Before long, they found themselves standing in front of God's throne. Nancy put on her best smile, and waited for a big welcome. God spoke to Sheila first. 'Welcome!' he said. 'Come in. After all, when I was hungry you gave me food, and when I was thirsty you bought me a drink. Then when I was homeless you found me somewhere to live – and d'you remember when I turned up without any clothes and you gave me some?' Nancy was horrified. God actually seemed to think *that* idea was amusing! 'Oh, yes,' he said, 'and of course when I was sick you came to see me – and even when I was in prison.'

Sheila's face was a picture. 'Me?' she said. 'I never even knew you existed. When could I possibly have done all those things for you?'

'You did them for other people,' said God. And whatever you did for them, you did for me.' Then a big door opened and an angel came and took Sheila through. Nancy couldn't see much but she could hear some amazing singing and it sounded as if a party was going on. How strange – having *that* kind of music in heaven – and parties!

Then God turned to Nancy. 'I hope you don't think you're coming in here,' he said.

'What?' she gasped. 'I've been at church

every Sunday since I can remember, I've always been clean living and responsible – not like some people!'

'But where were you when I needed you? asked God. 'Where were you when I was hungry, or thirsty? Why wouldn't you help me when I was homeless – instead of just shouting names at me? And what about that time when I was naked?'

Nancy didn't know what to say. The whole idea of God going around without any clothes on was beyond her! Then God went on, 'And the number of times I've been in hospital, or in prison, and I might as well not have existed for all the notice you took.'

Poor Nancy! 'I – I don't remember any of this,' she stammered. 'I've never seen you before – certainly not in *that* condition!'

'No,' said God, 'but you've seen my people like that, which is just the same, and you've done nothing.'

Nancy started to argue, but God stopped her. 'No arguments! he said 'No appeal – no strings you can pull.' And he was gone. Everything was dark and cold. Then Nancy could feel herself falling, and she closed her eyes tightly until she landed with a bump. 'This must be it,' she thought. Slowly she opened her eyes. Everything was dark, and there were strange shapes and grotesque shadows. Ugh! Then she heard a click and a voice said, 'This is the early morning news from the BBC.' It was Nancy's radio alarm clock! It had all been a horrible nightmare – so horrible that poor Nancy had fallen out of bed!

What a relief! Nancy got up and made herself a cup of tea. She didn't think she was half such a nice person as she had the night before. 'Perhaps there are more important things than being respectable,' she thought. She got dressed in some very practical clothes – the 'old' ones she wore for cleaning the house, which anybody else would have thought were lovely! 'Let me see,' she thought. 'Hungry, thirsty, strangers . . .,' and then she swallowed very hard, '*Naked* . . . sick, in prison . . . Where on earth do I start! need some advice.'

- Nancy *looked in the phone book*
- she *picked up the telephone*
- and she *dialled the number*

'Hello, Sheila – it's Nancy. Could I possibly come round to see you sometime?'

And quite a lot of people lived happily ever after.

Our Story

Draw attention to the display and explain – or let the children explain – what the different pictures represent. What other ideas do the wider group have?

Prayers

We're Sad

Please forgive us, God,
when we're too concerned with being good
to notice what other people need.
Forgive us for being unkind to people
just because they are poor, or merely different.
Help us to recognise you in other people.

We're Glad

Thank you, God, for not just staying in heaven
but living among us in this world.
Thank you for showing yourself to us
in the people we meet,
and in ways we never expect.
Thank you, God, for being a God of surprises.

Let's Pray for People

We pray for people who get pushed aside,
because they are poor, or sick,
or because other people don't approve of them.
And we pray for people like Nancy,
who miss out on the real joys of life.
Please God, help them all
to find you in one another.

Songs

God is making a wonderful world (WUW)
Out to the great wide world we go! (WUW)
Thank you, O God, for all our friends (WW)
Magic penny (A)
It's me, O Lord (A)
Make me a channel of your peace (A)
When I needed a neighbour (CAP)
The family of man (CAP)

Nancy's Nightmare
God's Story

Narrator   It was an ordinary night when Nancy went to bed, but next thing she knew she was in a very strange place.

Nancy   I've died. That's what it is. So this must be heaven.

Narrator   Nancy had always known she was a good person. She always went to church, never used a naughty word, always kept her home clean and saved her money. So she was not surprised to find herself in heaven.

Sheila   Hi, Nance! What're you doing here?

Narrator   Nancy was horrified; it was Sheila, her neighbour. She hadn't been near a church in forty years – and her house was always untidy. Well it would be: she was never there to clean it – always off helping at the night shelter, or prison visiting. Well, *she* wouldn't be getting into heaven! Nancy put on her best smile, and waited for a big welcome. God spoke to Sheila first.

God   Welcome! Thank you for feeding me when I was hungry and thirsty – and for helping me when I was homeless – and d'you remember when I hadn't any clothes and you gave me some? Oh, yes, and of course when I was sick you came to see me – and even when I was in prison.

Sheila   Me? I never did those things for you!

God   You did them for other people – people who seemed unimportant. And that means you did them for me.

Narrator   A door opened and an angel took Sheila through. It sounded as if a party was going on through there. Fancy having *that* kind of music in heaven!

God   Well, Nancy, I hope you don't think you're coming in.

Nancy   What? I've been at church every Sunday! I've always been clean and responsible – not like some people!

God	Maybe, but where were you when I was hungry, or thirsty? Why wouldn't you answer the door when I was a stranger – instead of calling the police and shouting at me? And what about that time when I was naked?
Narrator	Nancy didn't know what to say. The whole idea of God going around without any clothes on was beyond her! Nice people didn't do that kind of thing!
God	And whenever I've been in hospital, or in prison, I might as well not have existed for all you cared.
Nancy	I – I don't remember any of this. I've never seen you anywhere before – and certainly not in *that* condition!
God	No, but you've seen my people like that, which is just the same, and you've done nothing. No arguments, now! There are no strings you can pull here.
Narrator	Suddenly, he was gone. Everything was dark and cold. Nancy could feel herself falling, and landed with a bump. Slowly she opened her eyes. She could see grotesque shadows. Ugh! Then she heard a click.
Announcer	This is the early morning news from the BBC.
Narrator	It had all been a horrible nightmare – and poor Nancy had fallen out of bed! What a relief! Nancy got up and made a cup of tea, and began to think about herself. She didn't seem half such a nice person any more.
Nancy	Perhaps there are more important things than being respectable, and I'm going to start doing them. Let me see: hungry, thirsty, strangers, naked sick, in prison . . . Where on earth do I start! I need some advice.
Narrator	• Nancy *looked in the phone book* • She *picked up the telephone* • and she *dialled the number*
Nancy	Hello, Sheila. Could I come to see you sometime?
Narrator	And quite a lot of people lived happily ever after

'Are You a Friend of Jesus?'

Based on Matthew 26:30-39, 51-58, 69-75

BEFORE THE DAY

Can the children remember New Year resolutions they have made in the past? Ask them to write some down (anonymously) on cards and mark them 'kept' or 'broken'. Be positive about the broken ones – the point is to teach the children that failure can be acknowledged; perhaps some exemplary honesty from the teacher will encourage them! The cards can then be fixed onto a board, in two columns. Filter out any which might be specific enough for the child to be identified.

• Think about the actions for all the children to join in during the story.

ON THE DAY

Introduction

We're going to hear a story soon about one of Jesus' friends who wasn't quite so tough as he thought. First, we'll say our 'Thank you' prayer.

'Thank you' Prayer

Thank you, God, for all you give us,
thank you for the earth and sea;
thank you, God, for special people,
thank you, God, for making me.

God's Story

Peter was a very special friend of Jesus. He was one of the ones whom Jesus was preparing to carry on his work after he went away. Peter knew he would never let Jesus down. He told him so, as well. 'I'll always be your friend,' he said. 'Whatever happens, I'll be with you.'

Peter really loved Jesus – and he simply couldn't imagine that he might ever do or say anything to hurt him. After all, Peter was a brave man. He often had to go out fishing at night on rough seas, and of course he was sometimes frightened – who wouldn't be with the wind strong enough to blow away a mountain and the waves as high as houses? But he'd never gone to pieces, and he'd always kept his nerve and done his job. So he thought that he would always be rock solid in a crisis.

One evening, Jesus arranged to celebrate a special meal with his disciples, and afterwards, as they were walking, Peter heard Jesus say something very strange. 'You're all going to run away and leave me when things go wrong,' he said.

Peter was horrified. 'No, Jesus!' he exclaimed. 'I'll be right with you, even if I have to die.'

Jesus' eyes were full of love but also full of pain. 'Peter,' he said, 'I know you mean well, but by the time the cock crows in the morning you'll have said you don't even know me – three times.'

'Who – me?!' replied the astonished Peter. 'Never! I'm no chicken – I'll stick with you even if all of that lot don't.'

'Hey!' said Matthew. 'Who're you calling "that lot"? We'll all stick together, whatever happens, won't we lads?'

'Oh yes,' they all said. 'We won't fail.'

'Well, just stay here, all of you,' said Jesus. 'I'm going over there to pray.'

It was very late at night, and the disciples were very tired. They didn't mean to fall asleep . . .

'There he is! After him! Don't let him get away!'

There were soldiers everywhere. The whole place was lit up by flaming torches, and there seemed to be a riot going on. Jesus was standing calmly waiting for the guards to get to him. Peter decided to do something.

• He *drew his sword*
• and he *lifted it up*
• and he *brought it down hard*

Peter just missed the head of one of the attackers, and sliced off his ear. Jesus stepped forward in front of Peter, and said, 'No, that's not right.' Then he reached out and healed the man's ear.

Then Peter saw more guards streaming towards them. If they didn't move fast they'd be surrounded. 'Take cover!' he yelled and dived into the bushes, closely followed by all Jesus' other friends.

When they looked back, Jesus was tied up and taken away. 'Come on,' said James. 'There's nothing we can do here.' But Peter crouched low in the shadows, and followed to see where the guards took Jesus. Soon he found himself at the High Priest's house, where Jesus was put on trial. Peter sneaked in and warmed his hands by a fire in the courtyard while he listened. People were telling dreadful lies about Jesus, and trying to find excuses to kill him. Then one of the servants spotted Peter.

'Hey you!' she said. 'You're one of his friends, aren't you!'

'Who? Me?' blurted Peter in panic, 'I don't know what you're talking about.'

'Yes you are,' said someone else. 'I've seen you with him.'

'Not me!' said Peter. 'Never seen him before in my life!'

Then a third person said, 'I know you're one of his mob – you've got a northern accent. You're all the same you northerners – a bunch of dangerous revolutionaries.'

Peter was in a real stew by now, and he wasn't thinking before he spoke. 'Honestly,' he said, 'as God's my judge, I don't know him.'

It was then that Peter heard a terrible sound. Have you any idea what it was?

It was the cock crowing. The most dreadful sound that he had ever heard in his entire life, because he remembered what Jesus had said.

He'd let Jesus down! Jesus had been right all along.

Peter could feel the tears coming into his eyes, and he pushed his way through the crowd to get outside, where he collapsed in a heap on the ground and cried and cried and cried!

Peter learnt a lot from that. He learnt that he wasn't as strong as he thought. He learnt that it's best not to make rash promises unless you really know you can keep them. And a little while later, he learnt something really wonderful. He learnt that even when people let Jesus down as badly as that, they can still be forgiven and still be Jesus' friends.

Peter went on to be a very important disciple, just as Jesus had promised he would. But that's another story, for another time.

Our Story

Draw attention to the display, and point out that it represents 'success' and 'failure' (probably rather more of the latter!) Then ask if the children are going to make resolutions next year. The fact that we don't always get things right doesn't mean we give up trying. According to the bible story, God always helps us start again.

Prayers

We're Sad

We're sorry we're not always brave, Jesus.
We like being friends, but sometimes
it just seems too hard.
Forgive us for any times
when we've let people down,
and let you down at the same time.
Please help us to do better.

We're Glad

Thank you, God for all our friends.
Thank you especially for the really good ones
who forgive us if we get things wrong.
Thank you for showing your love
through our family and friends.

Let's Pray for People

We pray for people who feel alone
because they haven't got any friends,
or because they've been let down in the past.
And we pray for people who feel guilty
about letting their friends down.
Please God, give us all the chance
to start again.

Songs

Jesus had all kinds of friends (WUW)
Out to the great wide world we go! (WUW)
Thank you, O God, for all our friends (WW)
Where have all the flowers gone? (A)
It's me, O Lord (A)
The journey of life (CAP)

'Are You a Friend of Jesus?'
God's Story

Narrator	Peter was a friend of Jesus. He knew he would never let Jesus down. He told him so, as well.
Peter	I'll always be your friend. Even if I have to die for you, I won't ever let you down.
Narrator	One evening, Jesus arranged to celebrate a special meal with his disciples, and afterwards, when they were out walking, he said something very strange.
Jesus	You're all going to break down. You're all going to run away and leave me when things go wrong.'
Peter	No, Jesus! We'll never let you down. And even if the rest of them do, I won't – even if I have to die.
Jesus	Peter, I know you mean well, but by the time the cock crows you'll have said you don't know me three times.
Peter	Who – me?! Never! I'm no chicken – I'll stick with you.
Narrator	The other disciples all said the same.
Jesus	Well, just stay here, all of you. I'm going over there to pray.
Narrator	It was very late at night, and the disciples were very tired. They didn't mean to fall asleep, but fall asleep they did . . . until the noise woke them up. There seemed to be soldiers everywhere. Jesus was standing calmly waiting for the guards to arrest him, and Peter decided to do something.

- He *drew his sword*
- and he *lifted it up*
- and he *brought it down hard*

Narrator	And one of the gang found his ear had been cut off. Jesus stepped forward in front of Peter.

Jesus	No, that's not right. Let me handle this my own way.
Narrator	Then Jesus reached out and healed the man's ear. Peter couldn't believe it! All that stuff about loving your enemies was fine in theory, but Jesus should have known it was no way to handle this!
Peter	Take cover, everybody!
Narrator	Peter dived into the bushes, closely followed by all Jesus' other friends. They looked round just in time to see Jesus being arrested. They were very frightened, and ran off, but Peter crouched low in the shadows and followed to the High Priest's house where Jesus was put on trial. Peter sneaked in and warmed his hands by the fire while he listened to what was going on. People were telling dreadful lies about Jesus, and then some of the servants spotted Peter.
1st Servant	Hey you! You're one of his friends, aren't you!
Peter	Who? Me? I don't know what you're talking about.
2nd Servant	Yes you are. I've seen you with him.
Peter	Not me! Never seen him before in my life!
3rd Servant	Yes, you're one of them – you've got a northern accent. You northerners are all dangerous revolutionaries.
Peter	Honestly, as God's my judge, I don't know him.
Narrator	It was then that the cock crowed: the most dreadful sound that Peter had ever heard, because he remembered what Jesus had said. Peter pushed his way outside, where, he collapsed in a heap on the ground and cried and cried and cried!
Peter	I learnt a lot from that. I learnt that I wasn't as strong as I thought. I learnt that it's best not to make rash promises unless I really know I can keep them. And a little while later, I learnt something really wonderful. I learnt that even when people let Jesus down as badly as that, we can still be forgiven and still be Jesus' friends.

The Voice in the Wilderness

Based on Mark 1:1-11

BEFORE THE DAY

You can have some fun with this one! Make up a few large pieces of paper – as tall as one of the children. Cut a hole in each one to pass over the child's head, and on the front draw different types of clothes to represent very different 'images'.

• Think about the actions for all the children to join in during the story.

ON THE DAY

Introduction

We're going to have a fashion show in a few minutes, but first, we'll say our 'Thank you' prayer.

'Thank you' Prayer

Thank you, God, for all you give us,
thank you for the earth and sea;
thank you, God, for special people,
thank you, God, for making me.

God's Story

There was once a priest called Zechariah, who was married to Elizabeth. They had a son, John, who they thought was a real blessing from God – but there were times when they could find other names for him! John never combed his hair and he always went around in old, scruffy clothes.

One day, Elizabeth shouted at John, 'I'm fed up with you looking as though you don't belong to anybody!'

'There are more important things than looking good, Mother,' answered John – and found his pocket money stopped for a week for being cheeky. 'There are more important things than money, as well,' he said, and got sent to bed without his supper.

'What will the neighbours say?' moaned Elizabeth.

'Never mind the neighbours!' answered Zechariah. 'What will the *congregation* say?'

When John grew up, he didn't get any better. He seemed to be developing some very strange ideas. Worse still, he'd got some friends who thought the same. Then John started preaching. 'Repent your sins!' he shouted. 'Prepare to meet your God!'

The trouble was, lots of people seemed to believe John, and he spent days at a time at the river Jordan baptising people. One day, some of Zechariah's friends, who were also priests, offered to help. 'We'll talk to him,' they said. 'He'll listen to us.' So they put on their best robes and went to see John.

When he saw them coming, John pointed at them and shouted at the top of his voice, 'Ooh, you wicked people! You snakes! Don't come to me for easy forgiveness! You just wait until you see what God is going to do to you. You think you're so special, but you're not. God could make better priests than you out of stones!'

One of the priests, whose name was Levi, went up to John. 'Just who do you think you are? Elijah or somebody?' he asked. 'Perhaps you think you're a great prophet come back to life.'

'All I am,' said John, 'is a voice – a voice in the wilderness warning you of someone greater who is following me. Someone so great that I'm not good enough even to help him take off his shoes.'

Levi didn't get the chance to answer, because John was suddenly surrounded by people wanting to know what to do to stop God being angry with them. 'Share everything you have,' he said, 'and treat poor people fairly.'

'What about me?' asked Matthew, the tax collector.

'Charge people a fair tax,' said John, 'and don't fiddle the books.' Everybody laughed at that, because they hated tax collectors.

'What about us?' said some soldiers.

'Don't abuse your power,' John answered, 'and be satisfied with your pay.'

'And what about me?' asked a quiet voice. 'Will you baptise me?'

John stopped and stared in amazement. It was Jesus, the local carpenter. 'I can't baptise you,' John protested. 'You're good – it's you who should baptise me.'

Levi and his friends were horrified! How could John call this common carpenter good, after all he'd said about them? But while they were watching, Jesus went into the water with John to be baptised.

- When he came out, he *wiped his eyes*
- he *brushed back his hair*
- and *dried himself on a towel*

Then an amazing thing happened. It looked as though a dove was hovering over Jesus – but everyone knows that doves can't hover. That was the first strange thing, but it got stranger. There was a voice – a rather strange kind of voice, not quite like anything the people had heard before. Was it a man? Was it a woman? Was it a child? It wasn't shouting, and yet it could be clearly heard.

'This is my son, whom I love very much,' said the voice. So of course Levi thought it must be Joseph, but he couldn't see him anywhere. When Levi looked back, he was surprised because the dove had gone and everything seemed normal. Jesus was drying himself off on a towel, and John was talking to him.

Levi was puzzled. Had he imagined it all? He'd have liked to think that, but his friends seemed to have seen it as well. 'It must have been real,' said one of them. 'We heard it with out own ears.'

'Oh, that doesn't mean anything,' said Levi, 'I'm sure there's a natural explanation. After all, we're educated men, and we know better than to trust our experience.'

Even so, Levi couldn't help being a little worried as he and his friends went away to see Zechariah and Elizabeth.

'Well,' said Zechariah, 'what happened? Did he listen to you?'

'Had he combed his hair recently?' asked Elizabeth.

'I'm afraid it's bad news,' said Levi. 'He's obviously not going to listen to us, and he's got some really strange friends. I don't think we've heard the last of them by a long way.'

Our Story

Ask the model to stand at the front and 'dress' him or her in the various outfits, asking the children questions about the different impressions they create. You might ask whether they would trust the person, believe what they said etc., on the basis of the different clothes, and then make the point that the person wearing them is what matters. When a similar device was used in assembly, the staff were rightly horrified to hear a number of children say they would accept a lift in a car from someone dressed as a priest, whom they did not know. The speaker carefully pointed out that clothes alone are not a reliable guide.

Prayers

We're Sad

Sometimes we make fun of people
or refuse to take them seriously,
just because they are different.
Please God, forgive us if we've been hurtful,
or if we've missed something important
that you were trying to tell us.

We're Glad

It's good that we're not all the same;
what a dull world it would be!
Thank you, God, for people
who challenge us, and make us think.
Thank you for speaking to us
even when we're too proud to listen!

Let's Pray for People

Please God, help us to listen to you
when you speak through people
who seem to us to be strange.
Help both us and them
to realise how important they are.

Songs

I'm black, I'm white, I'm short, I'm tall (WUW)
Jesus had all kinds of friends (WUW)
Out to the great wide world we go! (WUW)
Thank you, O God, for all our friends (WW)
It's me, O Lord (A)
Water of life (CAP)
When I needed a neighbour (CAP)
He's got the whole world in his hand (CAP)

The Voice in the Wilderness
God's Story

Narrator	There was once a priest called Zechariah, who was married to Elizabeth. They had a son, John, who was turning out to be a real embarrassment to them.
Elizabeth	I'm fed up with you looking scruffy. Tidy yourself up!
John	There are more important things than looks, Mother.
Zechariah	Right! No pocket money for a week, for being cheeky.
John	There are more important things than money, as well.
Elizabeth	That does it! Off to bed with you – and no supper!
Elizabeth	What will the neighbours say?
John	What will the *congregation* say?
Narrator	As John grew up, he didn't get any better. He picked up some very strange ideas, and when he preached his father cringed in embarrassment.
John	Repent your sins! Prepare to meet your God!
Narrator	The trouble was, lots of people seemed to believe John, and he spent days at a time at the river Jordan baptising people. One day, some of Zechariah's friends, who were also priests, offered to help.
Levi	We'll talk to him. He'll listen to us.
Zechariah	Thank you, Levi. That's good of you.
Narrator	So they put on their best robes and went to see John.
John	Ooh, you snakes! You think you're so special, but God could make better priests out of stones!
Levi	Just who do you think you are? Elijah or somebody? I bet you think you're a great prophet come back to life.

John	All I am is a voice in the wilderness warning you of someone greater who is on his way. I'm not good enough even to help him take off his shoes.
Narrator	Levi didn't get the chance to answer, because John was suddenly surrounded by people wanting to know what to do to be better people.
John	Share everything, and treat poor people fairly. You tax collectors should charge people a fair tax, and don't cheat. And soldiers, don't abuse your power.
Jesus	And what about me? Will you baptise me?
John	(*Amazed*) I can't baptise you, Jesus – you're good – it's you who should baptise me.
Narrator	Levi and his friends were horrified! How could John call this common carpenter good, after all he'd said about them? But while they were watching, Jesus went into the water with John to be baptised.

- When he came out, he *wiped his eyes*
- he *brushed his hair*
- and *dried himself on a towel*

Then an amazing thing happened. A dove seemed to be hovering over Jesus – but everyone knows that doves can't hover. Then there was a voice – not quite like anything they had heard before. Was it a man? Was it a woman? Was it a child? It was very mysterious.

God	This is my son, whom I love very much.
Narrator	Levi couldn't help being puzzled and a little worried as he and his friends went away to see John's parents.
Zechariah	Well, what happened? Did he listen to you?
Elizabeth	Had he combed his hair recently?
Levi	I'm afraid it's bad news. He's obviously not going to listen to us, and he's got some really strange friends. I don't think we've heard the last of them by a long way.

Perfectly Willing to Learn

Based on Mark 7:24-30

BEFORE THE DAY

Consider different ways of learning: books, radio, television, computer disks, newspapers, even comics. Make up a display, using actual items and/or drawings. If in the course of this, any bright children say that we learn from each other, let that be the class's secret until the day of the assembly.

• Think about the actions for all the children to join in during the story.

ON THE DAY

Introduction

None of us is ever so good that we can't learn something new. We'll thing about that in a moment, but first we're going to say our 'Thank you' prayer.

'Thank you' Prayer

Thank you, God, for all you give us,
thank you for the earth and sea;
thank you, God, for special people,
thank you, God, for making me.

God's Story

Lydia hadn't got many friends. She was a very nice person, but she was angry about always being treated differently because she came from another country. One of her neighbours, a man called Andy, tried to help her with a little advice.

'You should try to be more like us,' he said. '"When in Rome, do as the Romans do."'

'You hypocrite!' Lydia answered. 'When you go abroad you behave just the same as you do at home – so why shouldn't I?'

'I'm sorry,' said Andy. 'Please don't misunderstand. I'm not prejudiced, you know. Some of my best friends are foreigners. I just think it would be better if you were all like us.'

'I think you'd better go, before I'm rude to you,' said Lydia.

It really did seem terribly unfair. Lydia was from Syria, as were quite a number of people in her district. They all lived in the same area because they felt safer that way. If they went to live anywhere else, people were rude to them. So they all lived close together in their own communities, and were accused of being unfriendly and not mixing! It really was a no-win situation, and you can understand why Lydia was angry – just like a lot of her friends.

Lydia's daughter, Ria, was a lovely little girl, just nine years of age, but she was very unhappy. When she tried to play with other children they bullied her. Then if she didn't try to play with them they called her a 'stuck up little Syro' and shouted nasty things like, 'Syroes go home!' after her. Gradually, she got more and more depressed, and wouldn't go out to play. Then she started locking herself way in her room and crying, and nothing anyone could do or say seemed to help. Lydia decided she really had to do something.

Meanwhile, Jesus had gone for a break. He was very tired, and needed time to rest, think and pray. His friends were even more tired than he was. So they found a house to stay in for a few days, and thought they would have a bit of a holiday.

Just as they were walking down the road towards the house, and dreaming of a nice drink, a hot bath and a long snooze, they heard a sound that made their blood run cold!

'Excuse me! Jesus! Over here! Sorry to be a nuisance, but . . .'

'If you're sorry, why are you doing it?' snapped Peter. 'We've had a terrible few days.'

'That's right,' said James. 'Go away and come back next week – or preferably next year.'

Lydia wasn't going to be put off half so easily as that. She had always had to fight for her place in the world, and she was quite capable of taking on a dozen or so men!

- She *wagged her finger* at Peter
- and she *shook her fist*
- and then she *snapped her fingers*

'I'm talking to the organ grinder,' she said. 'Not his pet monkey.'

That shut Peter up – he'd never even heard of an organ grinder!

'You can't talk to us like that,' said James. 'We're his special friends, you know. He's going to make us important people in his kingdom – our mum's arranging it, isn't she John?'

'Yes,' agreed John, 'so you just watch your manners.'

By now, Jesus had decided that he'd better do something. 'What's going on?' he asked.

'Oh, nothing important, Jesus,' said John. 'It's just this Syro woman who's making a commotion. Tell her to go away.'

Jesus looked at the woman, and asked, 'What do you want?'

'I just want my daughter healed,' she replied. 'She's full of all kinds of anger and resentment – not that I blame her for that – but it's beginning to get to her. Can you help?'

'I don't know,' said Jesus. 'I've got to provide for the people of Israel first. It's not right to feed children's food to the dogs.'

Now if it had been anyone else, they would probably have got the rough end of Lydia's tongue for saying something like that, but she was still hoping Jesus would help Ria. So she took a few deep breaths, counted to ten and tried again.

'Even the dogs get the scraps that fall from the table,' she said.

Jesus looked at her, and his face and his voice grew kinder. 'You're a shrewd one!' he said. 'All right – I'm sorry. You've persuaded me. Go on home, and you'll find your daughter in a much better frame of mind.'

He was as good as his word. When Lydia went home, Ria was a lot calmer, and together they found other ways of dealing with silly prejudiced people.

James couldn't get over the way Jesus had spoken. 'You let her change your mind, Jesus,' he said. 'Surely you're not admitting you were wrong – especially to a *foreigner*.'

'There's nothing to be ashamed of in making the odd mistake,' Jesus explained. 'Only in being too pig headed to admit it. I'm *perfectly* willing to learn.'

Then the disciples knew that Jesus really was a most extraordinary person.

Our Story

Use the display to encourage the whole group to think about ways of learning. Are there any others? What is missing from the display? Of course – we learn from each other! So we're all part of the display. If practicable, you might move the display into the main body of the assembly to emphasize the point. *Now* it's complete!

Prayers

We're Sad

It's nice to think we know everything,
but we don't of course.
Please God, forgive our pride
and make us more like Jesus;
willing to learn from others,
including people who seem to need our help.

We're Glad

Thank you, God,
for all the variety of people in the world.
Thank you for the things we can learn
from people of different cultures
who have experiences and knowledge,
as well as ideas to share with us.
Thank you for sending them to open our eyes.

Let's Pray for People

We're glad there are so many different kinds
of people in the world!
Please God, help people who are frightened,
who find differences threatening.
Help us all to live together
in this wonderful kaleidoscope world
which you have made.

Songs

Jesus had all kinds of friends (WUW)
I'm black, I'm white, I'm short, I'm tall (WUW)
Thank you, O God, for all our friends (WW)
Stand up! Walk tall! (WW)
Magic penny (A)
It's me, O Lord (A)
Sing a song of freedom (A)
When I needed a neighbour (A)
The family of man (A)
Black and white (A)

Perfectly Willing to Learn
God's Story

Narrator	Lydia was a very nice person; she was also angry about always being treated differently from other people because she came from another country. Andy, one of her neighbours, tried to give her a little advice.
Andy	You should try to be more like us. After all, 'When in Rome, do as the Romans do'.
Lydia	You hypocrite! When you go abroad you behave just the same as you do at home – so why shouldn't I?
Andy	I'm not prejudiced, you know. Some of my best friends are foreigners. I just think you should all be like us.
Lydia	I think you'd better go, before I'm rude to you.
Narrator	Lydia was from Syria, and the Syrians all lived in the same area. If they went to live anywhere else, people were rude to them. So they all lived close together in their own communities, and were accused of being unfriendly and not mixing! They couldn't win. Lydia had a daughter, whose name was Ria. Ria was a lovely little girl, just nine years of age, but she was very unhappy.
Ria	I hate being bullied! They call me a 'Syro brat'.
Lydia	Then don't play with them.
Ria	Then they call me a 'stuck up little Syro' – I can't win.
Narrator	One day, Lydia heard that the famous healer, Jesus, was in the area. Now of course, Ria wasn't actually sick – it was the unkind people around them who were sick – but Lydia knew that Ria needed a kind of healing, if she was not to be destroyed by her own anger.
Lydia	Excuse me, Jesus. Sorry to be a nuisance, but . . .

Narrator	Jesus was tired, and his friends tried to send her away.
Peter	If you're sorry, why are you doing it?
Narrator	Lydia was angry.

- She *wagged her finger* at Peter
- and she *shook her fist*
- and then she *snapped her fingers*

Lydia	I'm talking to the organ grinder, not his pet monkey.
James	You can't talk to us like that. We're his special friends, you know. He's going to make us important people in his kingdom – our mum's arranging it, isn't she John?
John	Yes, so you just watch your manners.
Narrator	By now, Jesus had heard the racket.
Jesus	What do you want?
Lydia	I just want my daughter healed. She's full of all kinds of anger and resentment – not that I blame her for that – but it's beginning to get to her. Can you help?
Jesus	I'm here for the people of Israel first. It's not right to take food from children and feed it to the dogs.
Lydia	Even the dogs get the scraps that fall from the table.
Jesus	You're a shrewd one! All right – I'm sorry. You've persuaded me. Go on home, and you'll find your daughter in a much better frame of mind.
James	Surely you're not admitting you were wrong, Jesus? Especially to a *foreigner*.
Jesus	There's nothing to be ashamed of in making the odd mistake – only in being too pig headed to admit it. I'm *perfectly* willing to learn.
Narrator	Then the disciples knew that Jesus really was a most extraordinary person.

Speechless With Surprise

Based on Luke 1:5-25, 57-64

BEFORE THE DAY

Ask the children for the titles of some of their favourite films, videos, books etc. Choose a varied selection and write them down on a flipchart in large letters. Write them also on small cards.

• Think about the actions for all the children to join in during the story.

ON THE DAY

Introduction

In a few minutes we'll hear a story about someone who had a big surprise; such a surprise that he was completely speechless – for a very long time! First, we're going to say our 'Thank you' prayer.

'Thank you' Prayer

Thank you, God, for all you give us,
thank you for the earth and sea;
thank you, God, for special people,
thank you, God, for making me.

God's Story

Zechariah couldn't believe what was happening to him! It had started just like any ordinary Sabbath day, with him going to lead worship. It was a very special honour, and only priests could do it. He had to go right into the 'holy of holies' as it was known, behind a curtain. No one could go there unless he was a priest – I say 'he' because only men could become priests, then. And you couldn't just decide to become a priest, either – you had to be born into the 'right' family! So Zechariah was very proud of the special job he did, and always tried to do it as well as possible.

This particular morning, though, he was a little bit distracted. You see, he and his wife, Elizabeth, were very unhappy because they didn't have any children. And they were even more unhappy because everybody seemed to think it was Elizabeth's fault. She must have upset God in some way, they thought, so that he had made her 'barren'. It simply never seemed to occur to them that it might be her husband who had the problem! Anyway, that was on Zechariah's mind a bit, as he began the ceremony in the holy of holies.

As he began to light the incense, Zechariah realised that he wasn't alone in the sanctuary – and he should have been! Out of the corner of his eye, he could see a figure standing by his shoulder. 'Whoever you are, you'd better go,' he said. 'You know only the duty priest is allowed in here.' Still the figure didn't move. 'Look, said Zechariah,' if you've got a problem see me afterwards and I'll make you an appointment to consult me – but it won't be until the week after next, mind you, and even then it'll only be an hour because I've got a lot of forms to fill in for the High Priest. Now I'd go if I were you before God strikes you dead or something.'

'Oh, I don't think he'll do that,' said the visitor. 'He doesn't often strike angels dead, you know. We've had the odd one that's fallen from grace, but that's quite another story.'

Zechariah was startled. He looked around, and sure enough the Archangel Gabriel himself was there.

'Well, knock me down with a feather!' said Zechariah.

'Not right now,' said Gabriel. 'I want a word with you. It's just to say that God's going to give you and Elizabeth a son. You're going to call him John, and he's going to be a really great man – he's going to prepare the way for the Messiah you've all been waiting for.'

'Is that what you've come here for?' asked the indignant Zechariah. 'Have you come just to tease an old man? Look, my wife's old. So am I, of course, but we men don't show it as much, do we? Anyway, we're too old to have children and that's it. And if we did have a child, he wouldn't be called John in any case. There've been Zechariahs in my family for generations, and no one has ever had a common old name like John!'

'Have you finished?' asked Gabriel. 'I hope you have, because that's the last word you're going to say for a bit. This is me you're talking to – Gabriel – Supreme Archangel, and trusted ambassador of God himself. I've taken more messages for God than your entire family's had hot dinners, and no one – no one, I tell you, has ever called me a liar before. No, it's no good trying to protest, because you can't talk – so for once you're going to have to listen. It's time you priests learned to do that anyway. As I said, you're going to have a son. You'll call him John, and he'll be a great preacher who will prepare the way for the Messiah. Got it? Oh, sorry, you can't speak can you? Well, that will give your congregation a bit of a break. Toodle-oo!'

Suddenly, Zechariah was alone again. The archangel had gone, and just as he had said Zechariah was completely unable to speak. Outside, the congregation were getting impatient because he should have started the service, and Zechariah had to try to signal to them that he'd lost his voice.

'He must have seen a vision,' said one of the worshippers.

'Rubbish!' said another. 'It's that incense that's got to him. I've said it before and I'll say it again, worship should be plain and simple without all that 'high synagogue' nonsense.'

Elizabeth had two shocks when Zechariah went home: to begin with he couldn't speak, and then he wrote her a note saying she was going to have a baby. She was overjoyed, and even more so when she found that her cousin Mary was pregnant as well.

By the time the baby was born, the whole neighbourhood was excited. Everyone was talking about it – well, everyone except Zechariah. And when the birth was announced the neighbours came round and they all sang hymns to celebrate – well, all except Zechariah. Then one of the neighbours asked, 'What are you going to call him?'

'We're going to call him John,' Elizabeth answered.

They were all amazed. 'Why John?' they asked 'You're supposed to call him after one of Zechariah's family. You can't call him John!'

Zechariah got a bit cross with the neighbours for laughing about it.

- He *picked up a pen*
- and he *dipped it in the ink*
- and he *wrote a note*

The note said, 'His name's John, and that's an end to it.'

'All right,' said Sam, his next door neighbour. 'No need to be stroppy.'

'I'm not being stroppy!' roared Zechariah. 'Hey, I can talk!'

Everyone laughed, and the celebrations began again. They went on well into the night, and this time Zechariah could join in properly.

Our Story

What must it be like not to be able to talk?

Invite children from other classes present at the assembly to take a card and try to communicate the title without speaking (or mouthing). The rest of the group have to guess, from the list on the flipchart, which title each child is miming.

Prayers

We're Sad

We're sorry, God, for not listening.
Sometimes we're so full of our own ideas
that we don't pay attention.
Then we don't hear what you want to say.

We're Glad

Thank you, loving God,
for speaking to us in lots of different ways.
Thank you, also, for people who listen well.
They show how much they care,
and how much you love us.

Let's Pray for People

There are people who can't hear at all,
and some of them can't speak.
Please, God, help them to take part
in the world we share.
Teach us how to communicate,
and help us make the world
more friendly towards them.

Songs

Rabbles, babbles (SS)
Out to the great wide world we go! (WUW)
Love is his word (A)
Make me a channel of your peace (A)
Peace, perfect peace (CAP)
I listen and I listen (CAP)

Speechless With Surprise
God's Story

Narrator   Zechariah couldn't believe what was happening to him! It had started just like any ordinary Sabbath day, with him going to lead worship. He had to go right into the 'holy of holies', behind a curtain. No-one could go there unless he was a priest – I say 'he' because only men could become priests, then. As he began to light the incense, Zechariah realised that he wasn't alone in the sanctuary – out of the corner of his eye, he could see a figure standing by his shoulder.

Zechariah   Whoever you are, you'd better go – before God strikes you dead or something.

Gabriel   Oh, I don't think he'll do that. He doesn't often strike angels dead, you know. Gabriel's the name.

Zechariah   Well, knock me down with a feather!

Gabriel   Not right now; I want a word with you. God's going to give you and Elizabeth a son. You're going to call him John, and he's going to be a really great man – he's going to prepare the way for the Messiah.

Zechariah   Is that what you've come here for – just to tease an old man? Look, my wife's old. So am I, of course, but we men don't show it as much, do we? Anyway, we're too old to have children and that's it. And if we did have a child, he wouldn't be called John. There've been Zechariahs in my family for generations, and no one has ever had a common old name like John!

Gabriel   This is me you're talking to – Gabriel – I've taken more messages for God than your entire family's had hot dinners, and no one – no one, I tell you, – has ever called me a liar before. No, it's no good trying to protest, because you can't talk – so for once you're going to have to listen. It's time you priests learned to do that anyway. As I said, you're going to have a son. You'll call him John, and he'll be a great preacher

	who will prepare the way for the Messiah. Got it? Oh, sorry, you can't speak can you? Well, that will give your congregation a bit of a break. Toodle-oo!
Narrator	Then the archangel had gone, and just as he had said Zechariah was completely unable to speak. Outside, the congregation were getting impatient because he should have started the service, and Zechariah had to try to signal to them that he'd lost his voice.
Worshipper 1	He must have seen a vision.
Worshipper 2	Rubbish! It's that incense that's got to him. I've said it before and I'll say it again, worship should be plain and simple without all that 'high synagogue' nonsense.
Narrator	By the time the baby was born, the whole neighbourhood was excited. Everyone was talking about it – well, everyone except Zechariah. The neighbours came round and they all sang hymns to celebrate – well, all except Zechariah.
Neighbour	What are you going to call him?
Elizabeth	We're going to call him John.
Neighbour	Why John? You're supposed to call him after one of Zechariah's family. You can't call him John!
Narrator	Zechariah got a bit cross with the neighbours for laughing about it.

- He *picked up a pen*
- and he *dipped it in the ink*
- and he *wrote a note*

The note said, 'His name's John, and that's an end to it.'

Neighbour	All right, no need to be stroppy.
Zechariah	*(Shouts)* I'm not being stroppy! Hey, I can talk!
Narrator	Everyone laughed, and the celebrations began again. They went on well into the night, and this time Zechariah could join in properly.

The Women's Story

Based on Luke 1:26-40

BEFORE THE DAY

Ask the children to think of 'special' people they know. Guide them away from choosing famous people such as film stars, politicians, royalty etc; or their school friends or family. They might think of a neighbour who shows them kindness, or perhaps a favourite babysitter. The children can draw and/or write about them, to make up a display with the heading 'Special People'.

• Think about the actions for all the children to join in during the story.

ON THE DAY

Introduction

We're going to think about special people in a few minutes, but first we'll say our 'Thank you' prayer.

'Thank you' Prayer

Thank you, God, for all you give us,
thank you for the earth and sea;
thank you, God, for special people,
thank you, God, for making me.

God's Story

This is the story of Mary. She lived a very long time ago in a town called Nazareth. Yes, that's right – that Mary. She wasn't very old – perhaps sixteen or thereabouts, but in those days girls got married very young, and people were beginning to talk. 'What about Mary?' they used to say. 'She's on the shelf you know – should be married and have a family by now.'

The trouble was that even people who didn't say that kind of thing sometimes still thought it, deep down. Where Mary came from, women weren't thought to be very important – and if they hadn't got a husband then they weren't important at all. But God was about to change all of that, as we shall see later.

Mary used to get upset, sometimes, about the cruel things people said about her, but the person she was really sorry for was her cousin Elizabeth. Elizabeth was much older than Mary, and married, and yet she didn't have any children. So of course, when people weren't gossiping about Mary they were being unkind to Elizabeth. 'Not much of a wife, is she?' they used to say. 'Can't even give her husband a baby.'

Mary was very sad about that, and every time she prayed she asked God to help her cousin Elizabeth to have a baby.

One day, Mary was doing some work around the house. There was a broken chair and she knew that if she waited for her father to mend it then it would never be done, so she went and found some tools and some glue and settled down to work.

• She *opened the jar*
• she *dipped in the brush*
• and she *brushed on the glue*

Just as she got to a very tricky part of the job, she heard a voice say, 'Hello, Mary.'

'That's strange,' thought Mary, 'I'm not expecting any visitors.' She didn't want to look up in case she let her hand slip and ruined her work, so she just kept her head down and carried on working. 'It must have been the wind,' she thought to herself.

Then the voice came again: 'Mary.' This time Mary knew it must be real, but she didn't want to lose track of her work. So she kept her eye on what she was doing, and said, 'Hello. Who's that?'

'I'm the archangel Gabriel,' said the voice.

Mary was just about to say, 'Yes, and I'm the queen of Sheba,' when something made her look up, and there he was! Mary was speechless at first. I mean, what do you say to an angel? Normally, she would have offered any visitor a seat and some food and drink, but she didn't know whether angels needed those things or not. Anyway, she hadn't finished mending the chair, yet.

When Mary eventually found her voice, all the words just fell over one another.

'Very pleased to meet you, I'm sure,' she said, 'I'm sorry that I ignored you just now, but I've just got to the tricky bit. If you want my parents, I'm afraid they're both out but if you come back about six you can see them, or of course you can talk to me but I'm sure you want someone more important. The Rabbi lives just down the road, and . . .'

'Mary! Mary!' said Gabriel. 'Let me get a word in edgeways. It's you I've come to see. I've been sent to tell you that God's very pleased with you. He thinks you're a really special person.'

'Oh, it's nothing,' said Mary. 'Anyone can mend a chair if they really want to.'

'Not that,' said Gabriel. 'You're going to have a baby. He's going to be a great ruler and save the world. He'll be known as the Son of God, and he'll rule for ever.'

Now if Mary hadn't known he was an angel she'd have laughed, but instead she just said, 'Me? Have a baby? That's a bit difficult for a single girl, isn't it?'

'Not for God,' said Gabriel. 'If God's decided to use you in a special way, why should he need a man to help him?'

'Well, it's usual' said Mary. 'At least where having babies is concerned.'

'Nothing's impossible for God,' said Gabriel. 'You know your cousin Elizabeth, who's never been able to have a baby?'

'Yes,' said Mary. 'Everyone thinks she's no good because of that.'

'It's certainly a very unfair world, isn't it?' said Gabriel. 'Women seem to get the blame for everything. Anyway, she's going to have a baby as well – she's six months pregnant. So don't you go saying that anything's impossible where God's concerned.'

Mary was a bit lost for words. Obviously something absolutely stunning was happening, and all she could think of to say was, 'Well, God's the boss – whatever he wants is O K by me.'

'Good,' said Gabriel. 'That's what he hoped you'd say.'

As soon as Gabriel had gone, Mary threw away the chair she was mending and all the bits fell apart again, but she was too excited to bother with mending a silly old chair! After all, any man can do that, but they can't have babies, can they! Mary went to get her coat and scarf, and then she ran out of the house and all the way to her cousin Elizabeth's place. They were so happy – they hugged one another, and they danced and sang, and were completely overjoyed. God had chosen both women for a special purpose, and no one could ever look down on either of them any more. It had always been a silly thing to do, anyway – hadn't it!

Our Story

Some people think that you have to be rich or famous to be special, but we know better! God uses ordinary, everyday people like us.

Prayers

We're Sad

Forgive us, please God, for silly prejudices:
for saying, 'That's a man's job',
or, 'That's women's work',
or even worse, 'That's a woman's place'!
Help us to give each other all the scope we need
to play a proper part in your work.

We're Glad

Thank you, God, for not being stuck
in the moulds we make!
Thank you for showing us
how silly they are!
Thank you for letting us be ourselves.

Let's Pray for People

Some people can't be themselves;
they always have to be
what other people expect them to be.
Please, God, set us all free from prejudice,
and help people to live in ways that please you,
and not just each other.

Songs

God is making a wonderful world (WUW)
God made the earth (WUW)
I'm black, I'm white, I'm short, I'm tall (WUW)
Jesus had all kinds of friends (WUW)
Out to the great wide world we go! (WUW)
Thank you, O God, for all our friends (WW)
Stand up! Walk tall! (WW)
Sing a song of freedom (A)
He's got the whole world in his hand (CAP)
The best gift (CAP)

The Women's Story
God's Story

Narrator This is the story of Mary. She lived a very long time ago in a town called Nazareth. Yes, that's right – that Mary. She wasn't very old – perhaps sixteen or thereabouts, but in those days girls got married very young, and people were beginning to talk.

Gossipper 1 What about Mary? She's on the shelf you know – should be married and have a family by now.

Gossipper 2 After all, having babies is what women are for, isn't it? And if she can't get a husband there's no way she can do that.

Narrator One day, Mary was doing some work around the house. There was a broken chair and she knew that if she waited for her father to mend it then it would never be done, so she went and found some glue.

- She *opened the jar*
- She *dipped in the brush*
- and she *brushed on the glue*

Just then, she heard a voice.

Gabriel Hello, Mary.

Mary Hello. Who's that?

Gabriel I'm the archangel Gabriel.

Mary Very pleased to meet you, I'm sure. I'm sorry not to look up, but I've just got to the tricky bit. If you want my parents, I'm afraid they're both out but they'll be back about six. If you want the Rabbi, he lives just down the road, and . . .

Gabriel Mary! Mary! Let me get a word in edgeways. It's you I've come to see. I've been sent to tell you that God's very pleased with you. He thinks you're a really special person.

Mary	Oh, it's nothing. Anyone can mend a chair if they really want to.
Gabriel	Not that! You're going to have a baby. He's going to be a great ruler and save the world. He'll be known as the Son of God, and he'll rule for ever.
Mary	Me? Have a baby? That's a bit difficult for a single girl, isn't it?'
Gabriel	If God's decided to use you in a special way, why should he need some man to help him?
Mary	Well, it's usual, at least where having babies is concerned
Gabriel	Nothing's impossible for God. You know your cousin Elizabeth, who's never been able to have a baby?
Mary	Yes. Everyone thinks she's no good because of that.
Gabriel	It's certainly a very unfair world, isn't it? Women seem to get the blame for everything. Anyway, she's going to have a baby as well – she's six months pregnant. So don't you go saying that anything's impossible where God's concerned.
Mary	Well, God's the boss – so it's O K by me.
Gabriel	Good! That's what he hoped you'd say.
Narrator	As soon as Gabriel had gone, Mary threw away the chair she was mending and all the bits fell apart again, but she was too excited to bother with mending a silly old chair! After all, any man can do that, but they can't have babies, can they! Mary got her coat and scarf, and then she ran out of the house and all the way to her cousin Elizabeth's place. They were so happy – they hugged one another, and they danced and sang, and were completely overjoyed. God had chosen both women for a special purpose, and no one could ever look down on either of them any more. It had always been a silly thing to do, anyway – hadn't it!

Questions! Questions!

Based on Luke 2:41-end

BEFORE THE DAY

Teach the class about different kinds of food, and prepare cards with 'You are a banana' etc. on them, along with a few facts to jog the children's memories on the day. Keep the cards safe until the assembly.

• Think about the actions for all the children to join in during the story.

ON THE DAY

Introduction

We're going to play a game of questions in a few minutes, but first we'll say our 'Thank you' prayer.

'Thank you' Prayer

Thank you, God, for all you give us,
thank you for the earth and sea;
thank you, God, for special people,
thank you, God, for making me.

God's Story

Joseph wasn't happy. He was tired, his head ached and his feet were sore. 'I don't know,' he said to Mary. 'Perhaps we ought to live a little nearer Jerusalem.'

'Oh, don't start that again,' said Mary. 'We like living in Nazareth, and it *is* only once a year we have to do it. Anyway, you must admit it was a great celebration, and Jesus loved it.'

It had been Jesus' first time at the annual festival. He'd certainly had a wonderful time, seeing all the sights of Jerusalem – such as the Temple and the Governor's Palace – and watching the big parades.

'Speaking of Jesus,' said Joseph, 'where is he?'

'Oh, he's with Zebedee and Rachel,' replied Mary. 'You remember, he spent most of his time with them in Jerusalem.'

'Well,' said Joseph, 'he's not with them now. Look, there they are – and there's no sign of Jesus.'

Mary and Joseph weren't really worried, but they thought they'd better check, so they hurried around, trying to find Jesus. Gradually they realised that he simply wasn't there.

'We'll have to go back to Jerusalem,' said Joseph, 'and me with these feet.'

'Well, you can't very well go without them, can you?' said Mary, a little crossly because she was a lot more worried about Jesus than about Joseph's feet.

So they walked all the way back again to Jerusalem. They could really have done with a good rest, but they were too worried to stop. On and on they walked, right through the night, with wolves howling around them and the moonlight making frightening shadows, and what with all that and being so worried about Jesus, Joseph almost forgot about his feet!

In the morning, they got to Jerusalem. 'Now where do we start looking?' wondered Joseph. It seemed like a hopeless job. For three days, Joseph and Mary hunted around the city and couldn't find Jesus anywhere.

• They *looked to the left*
• they *looked to the right*
• they turned and *looked behind them*

They went into the hotels and the amusement centres; they searched around the market stalls and checked all the stables, because Jesus loved animals. The only place they hadn't tried was the Temple.

So they made their way into the Temple, and straight away they noticed that quite a crowd was gathering in one of the courtyards. They pushed their way through the crowd, thinking that they might find a Temple guide who could help them to search, and guess what they saw!

In the middle of the crowd was a little circle of priests and teachers, all sitting around discussing religion (as you know, when people of that kind get together today, they tend to talk about religion – and use all kinds of long words to make themselves seem important – and things weren't much different then) and the little group were so engrossed in their talking that they didn't see Mary and Joseph pushing their way through. But Mary and Joseph had seen someone, though. Can you guess who?

There, sitting in the middle of the priests and teachers, was Jesus. He was listening very carefully to them, and asking questions. And they weren't just any old questions, either, but he was really making the wise people scratch their heads and think! Mary was embarrassed – rather like other parents often are when they think their children are being a nuisance – but was too relieved at finding Jesus safe and well to worry too much about that.

'There you are!' she said. 'What d'you think you're doing, making your father and me so worried about you? Four days we've been searching for you – and him with his feet as well!'

Jesus looked at her, and said, 'Why did you worry – you should have known where I'd be.'

Joseph was about to say something very stern to Jesus for being cheeky to his mother, when one of the teachers spoke to Mary.

'He's your son, is he?' he said. 'Well, he's a bright lad, and he's going to go a long way.'

'Yes,' said Joseph, grumpily. 'All the way back to Nazareth, and I hope his feet hurt as much as mine do.'

The teachers assured Mary and Joseph that Jesus had not been a nuisance. 'Never discourage him from asking questions,' they said. 'That's how bright children like him get even brighter.'

Mary and Joseph took Jesus home. They always remembered what the teachers had said, and encouraged Jesus to ask questions – even ones that sounded silly. And sure enough, he learned, and he became even wiser, and everyone said what a great man he was going to be one day.

Our Story

Call a few children from the class to the front, and give them each a card. The rest of the children must work out what each of them is by asking questions. You can then make the point that asking questions is a good way of learning.

Prayers

We're Sad

Sometimes we cause people who love us
to get anxious,
all because we don't think before we act.
Please, God, forgive us,
and make us more considerate.

We're Glad

Thank you, God, for people who care.
Sometimes we complain about it,
tell them not to make a fuss,
or that they worry too much,
but we're glad they care enough to worry.
Thank you, God.

Let's Pray for People

Every day, people get lost, and other people
   worry.
Sometimes it ends happily, sometimes it
   doesn't.
Sometimes it seems as though it will never
   end at all.
Please God, be specially close to people
who are separated from one another;
give them comfort, and hope, and if there is
   bad news
give them people to comfort them and love
   them,
the way you do.

Songs

Questions! Questions! (SS)
Jesus had all kinds of friends (WUW)
Out to the great wide world we go! (WUW)
Stand up! Walk tall! (WW)
In the bustle of the city (CAP)
Give me oil in my lamp (CAP)

Questions! Questions!
God's Story

Narrator	Joseph wasn't happy. He was tired, his head ached and his feet were sore.
Joseph	I don't know, Mary. Perhaps we ought to live a little nearer Jerusalem. At this rate we'll be ages getting home to Nazareth.
Mary	Oh, don't start that again. We like living in Nazareth, and it *is* only once a year we have to do it. Anyway, it's always worth the effort. You must admit it was a great celebration, and Jesus loved it.
Narrator	Jesus was twelve years old, and he'd certainly had a wonderful time, seeing all the sights of Jerusalem – such as the Temple and the Governor's Palace – and watching the big parades.
Joseph	Speaking of Jesus, where is he?
Mary	Oh, he's with Zebedee and Rachel. You remember, he spent most of his time with them in Jerusalem.
Joseph	Well, he's not with them now. Look, there they are – and there's no sign of Jesus.
Narrator	Mary and Joseph weren't really worried, but they thought they'd better check, so they hurried around all the other families who were walking with them, trying to find Jesus. Gradually they realised that he simply wasn't there.
Joseph	There's nothing for it, we'll have to go back to Jerusalem – and me with these feet.
Narrator	So they turned round and walked all the way back again to Jerusalem.
Joseph	Now where do we start looking? It's a big town, and it's full of visitors!

Narrator	For three days, Joseph and Mary scoured the city.

- They *looked to the left*
- they *looked to the right*
- they turned and *looked behind them*

	But they couldn't find Jesus anywhere. The only place they hadn't tried was the Temple.
Mary	He won't be in there. There are lots of things going on here that he'll find more exciting than religion.
Narrator	Even so, they thought they might as well try. So they made their way into the Temple and noticed a crowd in one of the courtyards gathered around a group of priests and teachers, and in the middle of them, was Jesus, listening very carefully and asking questions.
Mary	There you are! What d'you think you're doing, making your father and me so worried? Four days we've been searching for you – and him with his feet as well!
Jesus	Why worry? You should have know where I'd be.
Narrator	Joseph was about to say something very stern to Jesus for being cheeky to his mother, when one of the teachers spoke to Mary.
Teacher	He's your son, is he? Well, he's a bright lad, and he's going to go a long way.
Joseph	Yes, all the way back to Nazareth, and I hope his feet hurt as much as mine do.
Teacher	Never discourage him from asking questions. That's how bright children like him get even brighter.
Narrator	Mary and Joseph took Jesus home. They always remembered what the teachers had said, and encouraged Jesus to ask questions. And sure enough, he learned, and he became even wiser, and everyone said what a great man he was going to be.

Silly, Snobbish Simon

Based on Luke 7:36-end

BEFORE THE DAY

Prepare some posters such as 'Only blue-eyed people here'; 'Dark-haired people only'; 'Minimum height: X; 'Maximum height Y'* 'Only people who like jelly babies allowed' etc. and fix them around the walls before the assembly begins.

• Think about the actions for all the children to join in during the story.

ON THE DAY

Introduction

In a few minutes, we're going to think about some of the silly ideas people have. First, we'll say our 'Thank you' prayer.

'Thank you' Prayer

Thank you, God, for all you give us,
thank you for the earth and sea;
thank you, God, for special people,
thank you, God, for making me.

God's Story

Simon was a very important person. He was a lawyer and a religious leader. 'Everyone respects me in the town,' he said one day, 'because I'm friends with all the right people – and I'm careful never to be seen with any of the wrong ones.'

'What about Jesus?' asked his wife, Lydia. 'He's not one of your friends, and I think he should be.'

'You must be joking!' said Simon. 'He's an untrained wandering preacher, and he's got some very funny ideas about the law – he goes round encouraging people to break it, and saying God loves them even if they're bad. Why on earth would I want *him* among my friends?'

'He's very popular, and he might be useful to you one day,' said Lydia. 'Why don't you invite him round for a meal sometime.'

Simon wasn't really sure about it, but knew that Lydia's ideas were usually good ones. 'Anyway,' he thought, 'if I have some other clever people here – other than me, that is – we might be able to catch him out.'

Eventually, the day arrived, and so did lots of Simon's friends. 'Now don't forget,' said Simon, 'if he looks like winning an argument, change the subject.'

Simon and Lydia were so busy impressing their friends they didn't even notice that Jesus had arrived, until after he and his friends had sat down.

There was plenty to eat. Just about any kind of food you can think of was there on the table. Jesus and his friends were glad they had come.

• Jesus *peeled a banana*
• John started *eating the trifle*
• and Peter *drank some wine*

Suddenly, there was a lot of noise from the hallway; it seemed as though there was some sort of fight going on. After a few moments, the scuffling and shouting gave way to hysterical screaming, and then the door was flung open and in came a woman looking very upset. Simon thought she must have come to see him – after all, it *was* his house, and he *was* a Very Important Person in the town – but he wished she hadn't because he knew who she was. She was someone whom any self-respecting V.I.P. would never be seen dead with! But she ignored Simon completely and went over to Jesus. One of the servants was chasing after her to throw her out, but he seemed to catch a look in Jesus' eye, and decided to leave her alone. She didn't say anything at all. She just sat down by Jesus' feet and cried, and cried and cried. Before very long, Jesus' feet were really wet. The woman used her hair to wipe them dry, and then she opened a jar she'd been carrying and poured out some beautifully perfumed cream which she rubbed into them.

By now everyone had stopped eating and was staring at what was going on. Simon leaned over to his wife and said, 'You know who she is, don't you? She's thoroughly immoral – dreadful woman! This proves what

---

* (Choose; appropriate figures which will exclude some and include others)

I've always said about Jesus. If he were really a holy man he wouldn't let a woman like her touch him – let alone gush over him like that.'

The only person in the room who didn't seem worried by what was going on was Jesus. After a few minutes, when people were still whispering, he called out, 'Simon, can I ask you a question?'

'If you like, Jesus,' said Simon. 'Shall I have her kicked out first?'

'No,' said Jesus. 'Leave her alone, but answer me this. There were two people who owed their boss money – one of them just a few pence and the other thousands of pounds – but he told them to forget about it, and not bother to repay it. Now, who do you think would be most grateful?'

Simon was disappointed. He'd expected a really difficult question so that he could show off by answering it. 'Well, that's easy!' he said. 'The one who had been forgiven most would be most grateful.'

'That's right,' said Jesus. 'Now of course you don't think you've got anything to feel guilty about, do you? So you don't show much love, either.' Simon opened his mouth to say something impolite, but Jesus didn't let him get a word in. 'I walked over dusty roads to get here,' he went on, 'and you didn't even have the kindness to give me water so that I could wash – but this woman has washed my feet and dried them on her own hair! Come to that, you didn't even give me a proper welcome – you were too busy with your posh friends even to notice me – but she's been kissing my feet ever since she arrived. Now here's someone who has obviously been forgiven – and that's why she's so full of love. But of course, someone who's never even asked to be forgiven (mentioning no names of course) never really learns to love.'

Simon and Lydia were very careful never to ask Jesus to their house again; in fact they kept him at a safe distance from then on in case he embarrassed them even more.

Our Story

Get the children to move and stand around the walls, according to the posters. Are there any children with no 'home'? Could some of the children fit in more than one? Have any of the children got friends now separated from them in another group? Wouldn't it be silly if society was divided up in that kind of way? Really silly . . .

Prayers

We're Sad

It's not easy to admit when we're wrong,
and to apologise to people.
Please, God, help us to be humble,
to give people the chance to forgive us,
and to learn more about love.

We're Sad

Thank you, God, for loving us
even when we're not being very loveable.
Thank you for forgiving us,
and not being like Simon.
Thank you for being such a wonderful God!

Let's Pray for People

It's sad when people cut themselves of from others
because they don't approve of them,
and end up being sad and lonely themselves.
Please God, help people like Simon
to see the good in others,
rather than the bad.

Songs

I'm black, I'm white, I'm short, I'm tall (WUW)
Jesus had all kinds of friends (WUW)
Thank you, O God, for all our friends (WW)
Stand up! Walk tall! (WW)
Magic penny (A)
Love is his word (A)
Blowin' in the wind (A)
It's me, O Lord (A)
Black and white (CAP)
The family of man (CAP)
I come like a beggar (CAP)

Silly Snobbish Simon!
God's Story

Narrator   Simon was a very important person. He was a lawyer and a religious leader.

Simon   Everyone respects me in the town, because I'm friends with all the right people – and none of the wrong ones.

Lydia   What about Jesus? You ought to have him for a friend.

Simon   You must be joking, Lydia! He's an untrained wandering preacher, and he's got some very funny ideas.

Lydia   He's very popular, though, and he might be useful to you one day. Why not invite him round for a meal?

Narrator   Eventually, the day arrived, and so did a lot of Simon's friends. Simon and Lydia were so busy impressing their friends they didn't even notice that Jesus had arrived until after he and his friends had sat down.

- Jesus *peeled a banana*
- John started *eating the trifle*
- and Peter *drank some wine*

Suddenly, there was a lot of noise from the hallway; it seemed as though there was some sort of fight going on. Someone was trying to gatecrash the party!

Woman   You get out of my way! I want to see Jesus!

Narrator   A woman rushed in, ignored Simon completely and went over to Jesus. She didn't say anything at all. She just sat down by Jesus' feet and cried, and cried and cried. Before very long, Jesus' feet were really wet. The woman used her hair to wipe them dry, and then she opened a jar she'd been carrying and poured out some beautifully perfumed cream which she rubbed into them. By now everyone had stopped eating and was staring at what was going on.

Simon	You know who she is, don't you, Lydia? She's thoroughly immoral – dreadful woman! This proves what I've always said about Jesus. If he were really a holy man he wouldn't let a woman like her touch him – let alone gush over him like that.
Narrator	The only person in the room who didn't seem worried by what was going on was Jesus. Everyone else was terribly embarrassed, but he just sat there and watched what the woman was doing. He wasn't afraid, and he wasn't embarrassed. He knew why she needed to behave like that, and he was quite willing to let her do it.
Jesus	Simon, can I ask you a question?
Simon	If you like, Jesus.
Jesus	Answer me this. There were two people who owed their boss money – one of them just a few pence and the other thousands of pounds – but he told them to forget about it, and not bother to repay it. Now, who do you think would be most grateful?
Simon	Simple! The one who had been forgiven the most.
Jesus	That's right. Now of course you don't think you've got any need for forgiveness, do you? So you don't show much love, either. I walked over dusty roads to get here, and you didn't even have the kindness to give me water so that I could wash – but this woman has washed my feet and dried them on her own hair! You were too busy with your posh friends even to give me a proper welcome – but she's been kissing my feet. Now she's obviously been forgiven – and that's why she's so full of love. But of course, someone who's never even asked to be forgiven (mentioning no names of course) never really learns to love.
Narrator	Simon and Lydia were very careful never to ask Jesus to their house again; in fact they kept him at a safe distance from then on in case he embarrassed them even more.

Poor Ebenezer!

Based on Luke 12:16-21

BEFORE THE DAY

Organise a shop. Get the children to bring in a variety of goods for display, and make a list of their prices. Have other things without prices on the stall, too: a bottle of politeness, a box of love, a packet of friendship.

• Think about the actions for all the children to join in during the story.

ON THE DAY

Introduction

Most of us know the prices of some things, but do we know the *value* of what's really important? We'll think about that in a moment, but first we're going to say our 'Thank you' prayer.

'Thank you' Prayer

Thank you, God, for all you give us,
thank you for the earth and sea;
thank you, God, for special people,
thank you, God, for making me.

God's Story

Ebenezer was a very careful little boy. He had decided that when he grew up he'd be rich. He always saved his pocket money; he never spent it on what he thought were silly things like sweets or comics. And if someone was collecting for charity they never got anything from Ebenezer 'People should learn to look after themselves,' he used to say.

Ebenezer never had any real friends. No-one seemed to want to be friends with him. Sometimes he used to be sad about that, but then he'd say to himself, 'Friends are no use. Friends don't make you rich. I'm going to be richer than all of them.'

When he was a teenager, he never seemed to have any girlfriends, either. His parents got quite worried about it. 'Why don't you ask Rachel from down the road to go to the theatre with you?' his mother asked one day.

'What?' said Ebenezer. 'Have you seen the price of theatre tickets?' And he went to his bedroom to count his money. Ebenezer had quite a lot of money by now, but somehow it never seemed like very much. The trouble was that he'd got used to it. He didn't know what being rich really meant. He just thought that it meant having more than he had then, and so he was always trying to get richer!

Gradually, the people Ebenezer had been at school with got married and started families. He would have liked some children to play with, but he knew that families cost money. None of those people looked like ever being rich. So instead, he bought a farm and started growing crops. 'People will always need food,' he told himself. 'I'll get really rich selling my produce to them.' And he did. But he never *felt* rich, because 'rich' always means 'better off than I am now'!

Then one year he had a really big crop. Everything seemed to go right for Ebenezer that year. There was just the right amount of sunshine and rain, not too many slugs and snails and Ebenezer's home-made scarecrow kept the birds away. So when it came to harvest he had so much produce that he didn't know what to do with it! He had bags of wheat grain stacked up to the ceiling of his biggest barn, and so many apples, oranges and pomegranates that the greengrocers couldn't sell them fast enough. What was he to do with all this extra food?

While Ebenezer was wondering, the Mayor was on his way to see him.

• He *walked up the path*
• and he *knocked on the door*
• and he gave Ebenezer *a big smile*

Ebenezer was really pleased. The Mayor must have come to tell him that he'd been made 'Businessman of the Year.' This would show them! All those people who'd never wanted to be his friend would wish they'd been nicer to him, now. When he became Businessman of the Year everyone would want to be his friend, but he wouldn't let them of course. 'Too late!' he would say. 'Go away and leave me alone.' How he would enjoy seeing them squirm!

'I expect you know why I've come to see you,' the Mayor began. Ebenezer was very careful. He didn't want to look conceited.

'No,' he answered, 'I really can't imagine.'

'Well,' said the Mayor, 'you've had a really terrific crop, haven't you? You must be about the most successful businessman in the town.'

'What d'you mean, "about"?' thought Ebenezer. 'I'm *absolutely* the most successful businessman within a hundred miles!' He didn't say it, though, because he didn't want to sound conceited. So he just smiled modestly and nodded his head.

'So,' said the Mayor, 'we wondered whether you would consider . . .'

'Here it comes,' thought Ebenezer. 'Now I must try to look surprised.'

The Mayor continued, '. . . whether you'd consider helping out the poor people by giving some of your crops away.'

Ebenezer was just about to smile and say, 'Of course, my dear Mr Mayor! I would be honoured to accept the award,' when he realised what the Mayor had said.

'What!' he bellowed, 'You want me to give my food away? How will I ever become rich if I go doing silly things like that?'

'B-b-but you *are* rich,' said the Mayor.

'Nonsense!' roared Ebenezer. 'I've got to be a lot better off than I am now, before I'm rich.'

'What are you going to do with that food, though?' asked the Mayor. 'You haven't got big enough barns to store it.'

'Then I'll build bigger ones!' cried Ebenezer. 'I'll store up all the food so that I can get rich without having to work for it!' 'Just fancy,' he thought, 'suggesting that I should give my food away. Just because those silly people chose to have families, and wasted money on their friends, they expect me to help them when they're poor!'

That night, Ebenezer had a terrible shock. He died. No-one was there to hold his hand, and no one came to his funeral. Poor, sad Ebenezer died as he'd lived – alone. He never got to enjoy all that lovely food, and although he had more money than everyone else in the town put together, he never thought he was rich, because to him 'rich' always meant 'better off than I am now'.

Poor, sad Ebenezer!

Our Story

Draw attention to the 'shop'. Ask the children if there is anything they would like to buy, and then carefully check the price list. 'That would cost you 10p' etc. When it comes to the other 'goods' (perhaps with a bit of prompting) look very puzzled: 'There doesn't seem to be a price for this one.' You can then make the point that there are some ('priceless'?) things that money can't buy.

Prayers

We're Sad

Loving God,
we're sorry for the times we've been greedy,
when we've kept more for ourselves
than we really needed
and neglected other people.
Help us to remember that it's love
that makes us truly rich.

We're Glad

God, you are our friend.
Thank you for giving us
the most important thing of all.
Thank you for your love;
help us to share it with others.

Let's Pray for People

People like Ebenezer
will never be truly happy,
because however much they have
they just want more.
Please God, help people to be happy
with just enough,
and help us all to discover
the joy of friendship.

Songs

Jesus can make us truly rich (SS)
Out to the great wide world we go! (WUW)
Thank you, O God, for all our friends (WW)
It's me, O Lord (A)
When I needed a neighbour (CAP)
If I had a hammer (CAP)
I come like a beggar (CAP)
You shall go out with joy (CAP)
Love will never come to an end (CAP)

Poor Ebenezer!
God's Story

Narrator Ebenezer was a very careful little boy. All he wanted was to be rich. So he always saved his pocket money.

Ebenezer After all, if you look after the pennies, the pounds will look after themselves.

Narrator He would never lend anything to the other children.

Ebenezer Neither a borrower nor a lender be.

Narrator And he never gave his pocket money to charity.

Ebenezer People should learn to look after themselves.

Narrator Ebenezer never had any friends – but he didn't mind.

Ebenezer Friends are no use. Friends don't make you rich.

Narrator When he was a teenager, he never seemed to have any girlfriends, either. His parents got quite worried.

Mum Why don't you ask Rachel to the theatre with you?

Ebenezer What? Have you seen the price of theatre tickets? No, I'll just stay in and count my money.

Narrator Soon, Ebenezer had quite a lot of money, but he always thought that being rich meant having more! Gradually, his friends got married. He used to see them in their gardens, playing with their children.

Ebenezer I'd like some children, but families cost money.

Narrator So Ebenezer just had to resign himself to never having a family of his own. Instead, he bought a farm.

Ebenezer People will always need food – and they'll pay for it!

Narrator One year, Ebenezer had a big crop. While he was wondering what to do with it all, the Mayor called.

- He *walked up the path*
- and he *knocked on the door*
- and he gave Ebenezer *a big smile*

Ebenezer   (*Aside*) Oh, good! I bet he's come to tell me that I've been made 'Businessman of the Year'.

Mayor   I expect you know why I've come to see you

Ebenezer   (*Pretending to be casual*) No, I really can't imagine what you'd want with a humble person like me.

Mayor   Well, you've had a really terrific crop, haven't you?

Ebenezer   Yes, I have.

Mayor   You must be about the most successful businessman in the town, so we thought . . .

Ebenezer   (*Aside*) Here it comes. I must try to look surprised.

Mayor   . . . that you might give some food to the poor people.

Ebenezer   What! How will I get rich if I do silly things like that?

Mayor   B-b-but you *are* rich, Ebenezer.

Ebenezer   Nonsense! I've got to be a lot better off before I'm rich.

Mayor   But you haven't got big enough barns for all that food.

Ebenezer   Then I'll build bigger ones! I'll store up all the food so that I can get rich without having to work for it! What a cheek! Just because those silly people chose to have families, and wasted money on their friends, they expect me to help them when they're poor!

Narrator   That night, Ebenezer had a terrible shock. He died. No-one was there to hold his hand, and no one came to his funeral. Poor, sad Ebenezer died as he'd lived – alone. He never got to enjoy all that lovely food, and he never enjoyed being rich, because to him 'rich' always meant 'better off than I am now'. Poor, sad Ebenezer!

Airs and Graces
Based on Luke 14:7-11

BEFORE THE DAY

It's fantasy time. Let the children make themselves some simple fancy dress, based on a character they would like to be, whether from the real world or fiction. Keep it simple – a cardboard crown for the queen, coronet for lesser royals, a mask for Batman etc. Then on the morning itself, place some chairs in a prominent position, each labelled discreetly with a child's real name.

• Think about the actions for all the children to join in during the story.

ON THE DAY

Introduction
We'll be hearing a story soon about someone who thought he was more important than he really was, but first, we're going to say our 'Thank you' prayer.

'Thank you' Prayer
Thank you, God, for all you give us,
thank you for the earth and sea;
thank you, God, for special people,
thank you, God, for making me.

God's Story
Tom was really excited. He had been invited to the wedding of the famous concert pianist, Roland F. Sharpe to the operatic soprano, Edwina G. Flatte. They were a very loving couple, and everyone said how natural they were together.

• Tom *combed his hair*
• and he *tied his tie*
• and he *straightened his buttonhole flower*

'I've got to look smart,' he said. 'After all, I'm bound to be on the top table; I was an old college friend of Roland during my Academy days when I was a violinist.'

'Your "Academy days"?' said his mother. 'You're exaggerating a bit, aren't you? And you weren't a violinist, either.'

'Yes I was,' Tom insisted.

'You worked in the canteen,' said his mother.

'I'd have been a student,' Tom protested, 'but they just didn't seem to recognise my talent.'

'Couldn't seem to find it, more likely!' his mother corrected him. 'Now, Tom, you're not going to go giving yourself airs and graces are you? Without listening to any more that his mother was saying, Tom put on his coat and went out.

Meanwhile, in a different part of the town, Richard was also getting ready to go. He couldn't understand why he'd been invited. He used to work at the Academy, too, as the caretaker. Although he loved music, he'd never really been able to master an instrument, but he used to sit in his office at the college listening to music on the radio and loving every note of it. A lot of the students had very expensive instruments, and – although it wasn't really part of his job – Richard used to look after them for them sometimes, to save them carrying them around all the time. Roland never used to ask him to look after his piano for him. So he couldn't imagine why he'd been invited.

It was a lovely wedding; of course, the music was wonderful! All the most famous musicians were there, and after the service, Tom went around slapping them on the back, and talking about 'old times'. He thought it strange that such clever people had such bad memories, but he didn't mind reminding them who he was. Tom eventually decided to get off early to the reception.

Richard enjoyed the ceremony, too. He sat at the back, and thought how wonderful it was to be with all these famous people. Then after the ceremony he slipped quietly out to his car and drove to the hotel for the reception.

When Tom arrived at the reception, he went to the top table and sat down near to where the couple would be. 'Better leave room for their families,' he thought. 'Don't want to be pushy.' So he chose a place a few seats away from where Roland and Edwina would sit. Soon, he saw the happy couple approaching. Tom had his arm around someone – oh yes, it was that caretaker fellow, Richard. Tom remembered him from his 'Academy days'. Quite a nice man, but no musician – all he did was listen to it. Tom used to say, 'Any fool can *listen*. What's really hard is *playing* it.' You can see now why Tom never got accepted as a student.

Roland caught sight of Tom and came up to him, still with his arm around Richard's shoulders. 'Hello,' he said. 'I'm sorry, but I don't think we've met.'

Tom thought it was a wonderful joke! He roared with laughter, stood up and slapped Roland on the back. 'Hi there, Roly baby!' he shouted.

'Oh, yes,' said Roland, frowning. '*Now* I remember you. Look, I'm sorry – this is rather embarrassing – this place is for Richard here. You remember Richard, don't you. We always thought the world of him; he was so helpful – and *such* a musician! There's a place for you over there. Would you mind showing him, Richard – it's the one you were in before I found you.'

As Richard showed him to his seat, Tom didn't hear a word he was saying. He just had those words of Roland's ringing around inside his head '. . . and *such* a musician.' Roland must have got confused. Yes, that was it. Poor Roland – all the pressure of fame must have got to him. Then Tom noticed that the people around him seemed to be enjoying a joke. As he passed they started giggling and whispering to one another. Tom couldn't imagine what they were laughing at.

When he sat down, Tom watched Richard returning to the place he had wanted, and he noticed something very strange. Everyone seemed to know Richard, and to like him, and to want to talk to him. Although Richard was very shy, and found it a little embarrassing, people were grabbing his hand as he went past and smiling as they greeted him. Tom couldn't understand it, but then that was poor Tom's whole trouble, you see. He just couldn't understand what was really important in life, and what wasn't.

Our Story

Invite the children to put on their fancy dress and come forward to take the place prepared for them. As they come forward, ask them who they are, and then try and find their fantasy name on one of the V.I.P. chairs. It won't be there, of course, so you can say, 'I'm terribly sorry, there's a chair here for . . . (the child's real name), but that's not you, is it? Do the whole thing in a light-hearted way as the children learn that they have to 'be themselves' in order to get the places of honour.

Prayers

We're Sad

It's tempting to try and pretend
that we're something we're not.
Please forgive us, God,
when we give ourselves airs and graces,
and help us just to be ourselves.

We're Glad

God, we thank you
for making us as we are.
This is how you have made us;
and you love us.
Why should we want to be anything else!

Let's Pray for People

Some people are never satisfied with themselves,
and are always pretending,
trying to impress others.
Please God, help them to know
that you love them the way you made them.
And help us always to be kind,
and not to make people feel small
just so that we can look big.

Songs

Be yourself! (SS)
God is making a wonderful world (WUW)
God made the earth (WUW)
Stand up! Walk tall! (WW)
Love is his word (A)
Blowin' in the wind (A)
It's me, O Lord (A)
The family of man (CAP)
I come like a beggar (CAP)

Airs and Graces
God's Story

Narrator	Tom was really excited. He had been invited to the wedding of the famous concert pianist, Roland F. Sharpe and the operatic soprano, Edwina G. Flatte. They were a lovely couple, and everyone said how natural they were together.

- Tom *combed his hair*
- and he *tied his tie*
- and he *straightened his buttonhole flower*

Tom	I've got to look smart. After all, I'm bound to be on the top table; I was an old college friend of Roland.
Mother	That's the first I knew of it. When was that?
Tom	You know, Mother. During my Academy days when I was a violinist.
Mother	Your 'Academy days'? You're exaggerating a bit, aren't you? And you weren't a violinist, either.
Tom	Yes I was.
Mother	You worked in the canteen.
Tom	I'd have been a student, but they just didn't seem to recognise my talent.
Mother	Couldn't seem to find it, more likely! Now, Tom, you won't give yourself airs and graces, will you?
Tom	I told you, we're real mates, old Roly and me.
Narrator	Meanwhile, in a different part of the town, Richard was also getting ready to go. He couldn't understand why he'd been invited. He used to work at the academy, too, as the caretaker. Although he'd never learnt to play, he loved to listen to music on his office radio. A lot of the students had very expensive instruments, and – although it wasn't really his job – Richard used to look after them for them. Well, it was

	a wonderful wedding service, and afterwards Tom went around slapping everyone on the back, and talking about 'old times'.
Tom	It's strange that such clever people seem to have such bad memories, but I don't mind reminding them who I am. Well, better get to the reception.
Narrator	When Tom arrived at the reception, he was really pleased that he was such a special friend of Roly. There were so many tables!
Tom	I'm glad I got here early. Ah, this must be the top table. Better leave a couple of seats for their families – don't want to be pushy.
Narrator	Very soon, the room started filling up and Tom saw the happy couple approaching. Roly had his arm around someone – it was that caretaker fellow, Richard.
Tom	I remember him from my Academy days. Quite a nice man, but of course not one of the 'in' set. He was no musician – all he did was listen to it. Any fool could do that. What's really hard is *playing* it.
Narrator	You can see why Tom never got accepted as a student.
Roland	Hello. I'm sorry, but I don't think we've met.
Tom	Hi there, Roly baby! Love the sense of humour!
Roland	Oh, yes. *Now* I remember you. Look, I'm sorry – this is rather embarrassing – this place is for Richard here. You remember Richard, don't you. He was always so helpful – and *such* a musician! There's a place for you over there near the entrance.
Narrator	Tom couldn't believe what he was hearing. Everyone else seemed to find it very amusing, for some reason. Then Tom noticed something else that was strange. They all seemed to know Richard, and to like him, and to want to talk to him. Tom couldn't understand it. But then, that was poor Tom's whole trouble, you see. He just couldn't understand what was really important in life, and what wasn't.

Don't Be Taken In

Based on Luke 16:1-9

BEFORE THE DAY

Get the children to talk about the kind of people they would trust. They could draw pictures of, for example, police, doctors, nurses and perhaps even a teacher – this will be a very interesting exercise! Put the pictures up on a board for the assembly.

• Think about the actions for all the children to join in during the story.

ON THE DAY

Introduction

In a little while, we'll be thinking about trusting people. First, we're going to say our 'Thank you' prayer.

'Thank you' Prayer

Thank you, God, for all you give us,
thank you for the earth and sea;
thank you, God, for special people,
thank you, God, for making me.

God's Story

Jake was personal assistant to a man called Zebedee who was so rich that he couldn't keep track of all the money he had. Jake dealt with all the accounts, and made sure that Zebedee's customers paid their bills. One evening, he was sitting in his office counting up the day's takings: 'Two for Zebedee, one for me. Two for Zebedee, one for me. Two for Zebedee, one for me,' he counted. Jake was taking some of Zebedee's money for himself. He always did it, and his friend Mark, who was the butler, didn't approve. 'That's Zebedee's money,' he said. 'You've got no right to take it.'

'It's all right,' Jake replied, 'I'm worth more than he pays me, anyway.'

'That's not the point,' said Mark. 'He trusts you.'

'Oh go and polish your halo!' shouted Jake. 'Two for Zebedee, one for me. Two for Zebedee, one for me.'

Now Mark didn't like people who gossiped, but the more he thought about it the more convinced he was that he had to tell Zebedee.

Zebedee was not pleased, and he sent for Jake. 'I don't know exactly what's been going on,' he said, 'but I mean to find out. I've got to go away for a few days, and when I come back you and I are going to go through the books together.'

'Oh dear!' thought Jake. 'What if he sacks me? I'm no good at digging and things, and I'm far too proud to beg. Whatever am I going to do?'

- He *scratched his head*
- and he *wrung his hands*
- and he *put his head in his hands and cried*

Then he had an idea. He sent messages to everyone who owed Zebedee money and early in the morning there was quite a queue of people outside Jake's office. The first one in was a farmer called Luke.

'Tell me,' said Jake, 'just how much is it that you owe Zebedee?'

'Er – I'm afraid it's rather a lot,' said Luke. 'I owe him for a thousand gallons of olive oil.'

'My word!' said Jake. 'That's an awful lot of olive pips! Look, I'll tell you what, let's call it five hundred.'

'Well,' said Luke, 'it's very kind of you I'm sure. If ever there is anything you need – anything at all – you just ask me and I'll help you.'

'Thank you,' said Jake. 'I shall.'

Jake called the next person in. This was the local baker, called Sam, and he was very worried. 'Look, I know I owe you for that wheat,' he said, 'but you know how it is, what with the recession, and money doesn't buy what it used to – and my flour grinders have just gone on strike for better pay and free bread.'

'Exactly how much wheat do you owe for?' asked Jake.

'A hundred kilogrammes, I'm afraid,' said

Sam.'

'Don't worry,' said Jake. 'Let's call it fifty kilogrammes – would that help?'

Oh, ever so much!' said Sam. 'I'm really very grateful. If I can ever help you at all, you only have to ask.'

Can you see what Jake was up to?

The next person in was Dave, he wasn't at all happy about the wine bill he'd been sent.

'These prices are ridiculous!' said Dave. 'All that money for a few casks of wine – I'm not paying that!'

'I don't think you'd get the wine cheaper anywhere else,' said Jake.

'You must be kidding!' Dave objected. 'Why at one of the weddings I did, we ran out of wine and a guest made some more out of plain water. True as I'm standing here. Now if he can do that, how come you have to charge so much?'

'Well, I'll tell you what,' said Jake. 'Why don't we just mark your account as paid?'

Dave couldn't think of anything to say, except, 'Hmm! Well! Very good, I'm sure. Let me know if I can help you any time.'

This went on all day, and before long Jake had lots and lots of friends in the town. So when Zebedee came back he wasn't too worried.

'I've decided to leave,' he said. 'I'm taking early retirement. You'll find your affairs are all quite in order.'

'I doubt that very much,' said Zebedee. 'but since you're leaving we'll say no more about it. You're a thief, but for some reason I like you.'

So Jake left. He hadn't got a job to go to straight away, but he never starved because he'd managed to convince all the people in the town that he was a wonderfully nice man, and they all loved him and wanted to help him out. Everybody, that is, except Mark who knew exactly what had been going on. One day, Mark was talking to Luke, who said, 'Smashing chap, that Jake – really helped me out when I was in trouble.'

Well,' said Mark, 'he's certainly clever, I'll grant you that. But if I've got the choice between a clever person and an honest one, give me the honest one every time.'

And I think he was right.

What about you?

Our Story

Draw attention to the display. Can the wider group think of other examples? Perhaps some of them may question a few of the ones that have been chosen. Ask the children how they would feel if one of those people turned out not to be trustworthy. What harm would it do? (They might end up feeling they could trust nobody.) This can be used to emphasise the importance of not letting down people who trust us.

Prayers

We're Sad

Sometimes, God,
we think we're really clever
when we pull the wool over people's eyes.
We're sorry for being dishonest;
please forgive us, and help us
to earn the trust of others.

We're Glad

However many times we get things wrong,
you will never send us away.
Thank you God, for loving us so much,
and for forgiving us so often.

Let's Pray for People

We pray for people
who are afraid of losing their jobs.
Please, God, help them to trust you
and not resort to dishonest tricks.

Songs

God is making a wonderful world (WUW)
God made the earth (WUW)
Jesus had all kinds of friends (WUW)
Thank you, O God, for all our friends (WW)
Stand up! Walk tall! (WW)
Love is his word (A)
It's me, O Lord (A)
When I needed a neighbour (CAP)
If I had a hammer (CAP)
Make us worthy, Lord (CAP)

Don't Be Taken In
God's Story

Narrator	Jake was personal accountant to a man called Zebedee. One evening, Jake was counting Zebedee's money.
Jake	Two for Zebedee, one for me. Two for Zebedee, one for me. Two for Zebedee, one for me.
Narrator	You may think that's a strange way to count money, and Jake's friend Mark, the butler, didn't approve either.
Mark	That's Zebedee's money. You've got no right to take it.
Jake	Oh go polish your halo! Two for Zebedee, one for me.
Mark	Zebedee's a good boss. I can't stand by and see him being cheated by someone he trusts.
Narrator	Now Mark didn't like gossip, but the more he thought about it the more he knew that he had to tell Zebedee.
Mark	I hope you don't think I'm prying, sir, but do you actually know how much money you've got?
Zebedee	It's not your business. Anyway, I leave all that to Jake.
Mark	Well, I'd do a bit of checking if I were you, sir.
Narrator	Zebedee was not pleased, and he sent for Jake.
Zebedee	I don't know exactly what's been going on, but I mean to find out. I'm away for a few days, and when I come back I'm going through the accounts.
Narrator	Zebedee went away; Jake stayed home and worried.

- He *scratched his head*
- and he *wrung his hands*
- and he *put his head in his hands and cried*

Jake	Oh dear! What am I going to do if I lose this job? I'm no good at heavy work, and I'm far too proud to beg.

Narrator	Jake sent for everyone who owed Zebedee money.
Jake	Tell me, Luke, How much do you owe Zebedee?
Luke	Er – a thousand gallons of olive oil, I'm afraid.
Jake	That's a lot of olive pips! Let's call it five hundred.
Luke	Well, it's very kind of you I'm sure. If ever there is anything you need, you just ask me and I'll help you.
Jake	I'll remember. Now, Sam – how's the bakery going?
Sam	Look, I know I owe you for that hundred kilos of wheat, but I'm afraid I simply can't pay you.
Jake	Let's call it fifty kilogrammes – would that help?
Sam	Oh, ever so much! I'm really very grateful. And if I can ever help you at all, you only have to ask.
Narrator	Can you see what Jake is up to?
Jake	Hello, Jack – how's the catering trade?
Dave	I'm not paying that ridiculous bill for wine!
Jake	I don't think you'd get it cheaper anywhere else.
Dave	At one of the weddings I did, we ran out of wine and a guest made some more out of plain water. Now if he can do that, how come you have to charge so much?
Jake	Look, why don't we just mark your account as paid?
Dave	Fair enough. Let me know if I can help you any time.
Narrator	When Zebedee came back Jake knew he was going to give him the sack, so he resigned. All the people in the town loved him and wanted to help him out. All, that is, except Mark who knew what had been going on.
Mark	If I've got the choice between a clever person and an honest one, give me the honest one every time.

Ben and Neb get Better

Based on Luke 17:11-19

BEFORE THE DAY

What sports teams do the children support? Have you got a few rivalries beginning to emerge in the class? What about rock stars etc? You should soon get a pretty lively discussion going. Divide the class into two groups, such as Reds and Blues and get them to make placards with slogans on saying things like, 'Reds are Greatest', 'Blues are Best' etc. You will need to persuade a few volunteers, perhaps including teachers, to take the key parts on the day.

• Think about the actions for all the children to join in during the story.

ON THE DAY

Introduction

We've got a story to listen to in a few minutes, but first we're going to say our 'Thank you' prayer.

'Thank you' Prayer

Thank you, God, for all you give us,
thank you for the earth and sea;
thank you, God, for special people,
thank you, God, for making me.

God's Story

I want to introduce you to two friends, called Ben and Neb. Neb had been named after a famous Persian king, who had a very long name that no one could pronounce properly – so they just shortened it to Neb. Although Ben and Neb were great friends, they were as opposite as their names. Ben was from Galilee and Neb was from the next county, called Samaria. And as a rule the people of those two counties liked each other about as much as supporters of Manchester United and Aston Villa! They each thought the other worshipped the wrong God. Ben and Neb had a very nasty disease. Everybody was afraid of catching it, and so they drove Ben and Neb away to live right on the border between the two counties so that whenever anybody started throwing stones at them they could just nip across the border and get away. Of course, it got a bit difficult if people from both counties were doing it at the same time!

One day, Ben and Neb met up with eight other people like themselves. One of them, whose name was Rachel, said, 'We've heard about a man called Jesus who heals people, and we're going to find him.' After a few days, they saw a man walking along the road towards them with a lot of other people around him. Rachel saw some faces she knew. 'That's Jesus,' she said.

'He's not going to want to know us,' said Ben. 'Look, he's got all his friends round him.'

Neb thought it was worth trying, anyway. 'Why don't we just shout to him from where we are?' he suggested.

'Fair enough,' said Rachel, and she started shouting. 'Hey, Jesus! Can you help us?'

Jesus called back, 'Go and show yourselves to the priests.' That was because in those days the priests were very important, and they had to say it was okay for people who'd been chased away to come back.

Ben was disappointed. 'Fat lot of good that is!' he complained. 'It's the priests who put us here in the first place.'

'Come on,' said Rachel. 'Trust me! Sorry – I meant trust Jesus.' And off they all went towards the city. As they were walking along, though, Ben started thinking, 'I bet Jesus is having a good laugh at us.' He went up to Rachel and started shouting at her about how silly and how humiliating it all was.

- He *waved his arms*
- and he *thumped his palm*
- and he *wagged his finger in* Rachel's face

'I'm not going to let Jesus make a fool of me,' he yelled.

Rachel wasn't listening to Ben; she was staring at the finger that was being waved in front of her. 'Hey, Ben!' she shouted. 'Look at your finger!'

'Don't change the subject!' roared Ben.

'No, really!' Rachel insisted. 'Look – the skin's healthy. And your face as well.'

Ben stopped yelling and looked. It was true. Then he said to Rachel, 'Your face is better, too.' And before long, they were all jumping up and down for joy, because they realised they had been healed.'

'Come on,' said Rachel. 'Let's go to the priests.'

'Shouldn't we go and thank Jesus, first?' asked Neb, but Rachel and the others were too excited to listen.

So off they went – or at least, nine of them did. Neb just said, 'I'll catch you later,' and went off to find Jesus. When he found him he went rushing up to say thank you.

Jesus turned to his disciples, and said, 'Isn't that interesting? Ten were healed, but only one says thank you – and he's the last one you'd have expected to. You know, the people who are called "outsiders" are often the ones with real faith.'

Our Story

Divide up the assembly into two halves, using the placards. Don't worry if the sides aren't even; it doesn't matter at all. Place the two groups at either side of the hall with a line down the middle; blindfold the volunteers and challenge them to walk up the line. If they stray to one side or the other, then that group must shout at them until they resume their precarious middle path. Of course, if they overcorrect, then the other crowd of children will take over!

That was how it was for people like Ben and Neb, forced to live on the border because neither side would have them. Horrible, isn't it? Depending on the circumstances, there are various contemporary points which could be brought out of this.

Prayers

We're Sad

People are often very kind to us,
and we don't notice.
Or we forget to say 'Thank you'.
We're sorry, God. Please forgive us,
and teach us to appreciate each other.

We're Glad

We often hear what a dreadful world this is,
but it's still full of wonderful people!
Sometimes, we get kindnesses.
from people from whom we don't expect it.
Thank you, God, for lovely surprises!

Let's Pray for People

Some people suffer from diseases
which other people find frightening.
So they get pushed away and feel lonely.
Please God, help us to be kind to people
who need friendship most,
and help us not to be afraid.

Songs

Jesus can make us truly rich (SS)
Jesus had all kinds of friends (WUW)
Out to the great wide world we go! (WUW)
Stand up! Walk tall! (WW)
Make me a channel of your peace (A)
When I needed a neighbour (CAP)
The family of man (CAP)
If I had a hammer (CAP)

Ben and Neb get Better
God's Story

Narrator	I want to introduce you to two friends, called Ben and Neb. They were as opposite as their names. Ben was from Galilee and Neb was from the next county, called Samaria. Their problem was that they had a very nasty disease which made them come out in a rash all over. Everybody was afraid of catching it, and so they drove Ben and Neb away. They didn't belong anywhere, and they lived right on the border so that whenever anybody started throwing stones at them they could just nip across the border and get away. One day, Ben and Neb met up with some other people like themselves. There were eight of them, including a woman called Rachel.
Rachel	We're looking for Jesus. He heals people.
Narrator	Ben and Neb joined up with Rachel and her group, and soon they saw Jesus who was with his friends.
Neb	He won't want to know – not with his friends around.
Rachel	I had a friend called Joe once, who was worse than any of us, and Jesus touched him.
Ben	You're the one that's touched if you believe that!
Rachel	You can scoff if you like, but it's true. Joe told me himself.
Neb	Why don't we just shout to him from where we are? Then if he doesn't want to get too close he can say so.
Rachel	Fair enough. Hey, Jesus! Over here! Can you help us?
Jesus	Go and show yourselves to the priests.
Ben	Fat lot of good that is! The priests put us here in the first place – they'll just chase us away again.
Rachel	Just a minute – I think I know what it's about. Let's go.

Neb	Don't be silly, there's no point.
Rachel	Yes there is. Trust me! Sorry – I meant trust Jesus.
Narrator	Rachel set off, and gradually the rest followed
Ben	I bet Jesus is having a good laugh at us – and I'm not being made a fool of by anyone.
Narrator	Ben was very angry, and as he spoke:

- he *waved his arms*
- and he *thumped his palm*
- and he *wagged his finger* in Rachel's face

Rachel	Hey, Ben! Look at your finger!
Ben	Don't change the subject!
Rachel	No, really! Look – the skin's healthy. And your face as well.
Narrator	Ben stopped yelling and looked. It was true. His hands and arms were healthy as though he'd been given a completely new skin.
Ben	Your face is better, too. We've all been healed!
Rachel	Come on, let's go to the priests.
Neb	Shouldn't we go and thank Jesus, first?
Rachel	Oh, he'll be long gone by now.
Ben	Anyway, the priests are far more important than Jesus.
Narrator	So off they went – or at least, nine of them did. Neb went back and found Jesus, and thanked him.
Jesus	Isn't that interesting? Ten were healed, but only one says thank you – and he's the last one you'd have expected to. You know, the people who are called 'outsiders' are often the ones with real faith.

Keep Your Wig On, Judge!

Based on Luke 18:2-5

BEFORE THE DAY

Take the class to a suitable part of the school, and tell them to be very quiet and listen. Get them to draw what they hear: traffic on the road outside; footsteps in the corridor; lessons going on in other classes; kitchen staff preparing the school lunch; telephones ringing – and how many will notice the sound of pencils on paper right next to them? How long can the silence creatively be maintained? Collect in the drawings and make a display.

• Think about the actions for all the children to join in during the story.

ON THE DAY

Introduction

Some of the children have been doing some careful listening this week, and they're going to tell us about it. But first, we're going to say our 'Thank you' prayer.

'Thank you' Prayer

Thank you, God, for all you give us,
thank you for the earth and sea;
thank you, God, for special people,
thank you, God, for making me.

God's Story

Gabriella's husband had died and she was left alone with her daughter, Becky. In those days women's jobs were not very well paid, and anyway, Gabriella couldn't leave Becky on her own while she went to work. So how were they going to pay the rent?

Sam, the landlord, was one of those people who was always very nice to anyone who had money to spend, but changed completely if they fell on hard times. 'It's not my fault your husband's dead, is it?' he said, nastily. 'I've still got to live you know. I've got to pay my butler, and the man who prunes my roses, and of course I only drink the very best wine. So I can't go reducing people's rent or I might end up poor and pathetic like you.'

Gabriella didn't know what to do. For a time she got a job fig-picking, but she knew that once the season was over that would come to an end. Then she heard about a job as a cleaner at the local tailor's. The work was quite hard – Gabriella was always getting hurt by needles and scissors that were left lying around – and it was very badly paid. Also, she had to take Becky along with her, and she didn't think that was either safe or fair.

One day Becky said to her mother, 'If you didn't have to pay so much rent, you wouldn't need to earn so much money.'

Gabriella smiled. 'The trouble is,' she explained, 'that Sam owns most of the houses in the town and can charge what he likes.'

That afternoon, when they were out for a walk, they saw a man who was wearing really funny clothes, and a wig. 'Hasn't he got any hair of his own?' asked Becky.

'Yes,' laughed Gabriella, 'but he's a very important person. He's a judge.'

'Oh,' said Becky. 'Does that mean that the more important people are, the more silly they have to look?'

Gabriella thought that Becky might have a point, but she was teaching her daughter to be polite, so she said, 'You mustn't talk like that about people. He probably thinks that your clothes are silly, but he hasn't said so.'

'What does a judge do, then?' asked Becky.

'Oh,' said her mother, 'he settles arguments between people. If someone's being unfair to someone else then he can tell them to stop.'

Before Gabriella could stop her, Becky was running over to the judge.

'Hey, Mister Judgy Person,' she called out. 'Can you help my mum, please and stop her landlord charging her so much rent? – and I promise I won't say your wig looks silly ever again.'

The judge stopped. 'Is this abominable child your responsibility?' he shouted. 'Take her home and punish her – and teach her to be polite to important people, you disgusting, scruffy woman.'

'She's not abominable,' said Gabriella, 'and if I'm scruffy it's because I do an honest job. Anyway, I'd rather be scruffy than rude and arrogant. Come on, Becky.'

Gabriella was surprised at herself. 'I shouldn't have done that,' she said to Becky. 'We must always be polite. Just because someone's rude to you doesn't mean you can be rude back.'

'You weren't rude,' said Becky. 'You were just standing up for yourself. Anyway, I think he should help you.'

Gabriella started thinking about what Becky had said. Perhaps she should go and see the judge.

'Why should I help you?' said the judge. 'You're the rude woman with the horrible child, aren't you?'

'I'm sorry if you think I was rude,' Becky answered, 'but you weren't very polite, either. Anyway what you think of me doesn't alter the case. I'm being charged too much rent.'

'Go away,' said the judge. 'Sam is a good respectable citizen. And he's very rich. We need rich people in this town a lot more than we need poor spongers like you.'

That did it. Gabriella decided the judge was going to do the right thing. Every day, she went to his house and knocked on his door, but he wouldn't see her. Then she made a big poster saying 'Sack the unjust judge' and stood outside his courtroom with it. Soon she was joined by other women, and every time the judge went past they started chanting.

- *Fair rents for all!*
- *Fair rents for all!*
- *etc.*

Eventually, it all got too much for the judge, and he called Sam to see him.

'You'll have to lower your rents,' he said.

'Not me,' said Sam. 'Anyway, if I do that I'll have less to give to you.'

'Shut up!' hissed the judge. 'D'you want the whole town to know that you bribe me? Look, either you reduce your rents or we'll get the inspectors in to check your houses over.'

'Oh, don't do that!' said Sam, hastily. 'I'll cut the rents.'

The judge went and told the women. 'Now will you leave me alone?' he asked.

'Well,' replied Gabriella,' we're very pleased about the rents, but we think we ought to talk to you about fair wages for cleaners.'

Our Story

Draw attention to the display and show the children what a range of noises is around them all the time. Life is a lot more interesting if we learn to listen!

Prayers

We're Sad

Sometimes, we're a bit like that judge:
We know what we should do,
but we try to get out of it.
Please forgive us, God,
and make us more willing to help people.

We're Glad

Thank you, God, for not having to be pestered.
Thank you for listening to us,
and for caring about us.

Let's Pray for People

There are lots of people like Gabriella,
who have to fight for fair treatment.
Loving God, please help us to care more,
to listen better,
and to make the world more fair
without waiting to be pestered into it.

Songs

Life for the poor was hard and tough (WUW)
Out to the great wide world we go! (WUW)
Stand up! Walk tall! (WW)
Magic penny (A)
Sing a song of freedom (A)
I come like a beggar (CAP)
Love will never come to an end (CAP)
Lord of the dance (CAP)
If I had a hammer (CAP)

Keep Your Wig On, Judge!
God's Story

Narrator Gabriella's husband had died and she was left alone with her daughter, Becky and with no money. Sam, the greedy landlord, wasn't very nice about it.

Sam It's not my fault your husband's dead. If I reduce the rent I might end up poor and pathetic like you.

Narrator Gabriella didn't know what to do. Then she got a job as a cleaner. The work was quite hard and very badly paid. Becky thought it was all Sam's fault.

Becky If you paid less rent, you'd need less money.

Gabriella Sam owns all the houses, so he can set his own rents.

Narrator That afternoon, when they were out for a walk, they saw a man who was wearing really funny clothes.

Becky Why's he wearing a wig? Hasn't he any hair?

Gabriella Yes, but he's a very important person. He's a judge.

Becky Oh, do important people have to look silly?

Gabriella You mustn't talk like that about people.

Becky What does a judge do, then?

Gabriella He settles arguments and makes people behave fairly.

Becky Hey, Mister Judgy Person, can you help my mum, and stop her landlord charging so much rent? – and I promise I won't say your wig looks silly ever again.

Judge Take this abominable child home and teach her to be polite to important men, you dreadful, scruffy woman.

Gabriella She's not abominable, and I work for my living. I'd rather be scruffy than rude. Come on, Becky.

Narrator Gabriella was surprised at herself.

Gabriella	I shouldn't have done that. Just because someone's rude doesn't mean it's right to be rude back.
Becky	Well, I think he should help you.
Gabriella	You may be right. I'll go and see him one day.
Judge	Why should I help you? You and your horrible child!
Gabriella	That's not the point. Sam's charging too much rent.
Judge	Go away, Sam is a good respectable citizen. And he's very rich. We need rich people in this town a lot more than we need poor spongers like you.
Narrator	Gabriella decided the judge was going to do the right thing, whatever it took. Every day, she went and hammered on his door. Then she stood outside with a big poster saying, 'Sack the unjust judge'. Soon other women joined her and started chanting,

- *Fair rents for all*
- *Fair rents for all*
- *etc.*

Eventually, the judge called Sam to see him.

Judge	You'll have to lower your rents.
Sam	If I do that you'll have to reduce your cut.
Judge	Shut up! D'you want the whole town to hear? Look, I've had enough of being pestered by this woman. Either you reduce your rents or we'll get the inspectors in to check your houses over.
Sam	Oh, don't do that! I'll cut the rents.
Judge	Now will you women leave me alone?
Gabriella	Well, we're very pleased about the rents, but we think we ought to talk to you about fair wages for cleaners.

Representation and Reality

Based on Luke 18:9-14

BEFORE THE DAY

Ask the children to write some letters to God; simple little notes containing just one sentence either of praise or perhaps to pray for someone who is unwell. Pin the letters up, where appropriate, on a display board.

• Think about the actions for all the children to join in during the story.

ON THE DAY

Introduction

This morning we're going to think about ways of praying. First, we'll say our 'Thank you' prayer.

'Thank you' Prayer

Thank you, God, for all you give us,
thank you for the earth and sea;
thank you, God, for special people,
thank you, God, for making me.

God's Story

'Oh, dear, it's Sunday again,' thought Tony, and he felt guilty straight away because everyone kept telling him that Christians should enjoy Sundays: going to church, worshipping God, seeing other Christian people. *Real* Christians, Tony thought, enjoyed all of that – so what was wrong with him?

He expected that Harry Snooks would be there, as usual. Harry was a Real Christian: a fully paid up, card-carrying member of the Perfectly Pious True Believers' Club. He was so good it hurt! Everyone knew how good Harry was, because Harry was always telling them. Every year he sat down and worked out how much money he'd earned, and gave exactly one tenth of it to the church. Each week, he was at the Prayer Meeting, the Bible Study, the Praise Meeting and the 'Let's Spread the Gospel' Club – known among a few irreverents as Bible Bashers Anonymous, which would have infuriated Harry if he'd ever found out.

What Tony most dreaded about going to church was the slot in the service where anyone could pray out loud. Of course, Harry *always* prayed, and sounded so eloquent, using long words and mysterious phrases like 'substitutionary atonement'. Tony always felt he ought to pray like that, but he could never compete. Not that he hadn't tried, though. There was that Sunday when he'd joined in. He'd spent most of Saturday writing his own prayer out, going over it again and again and changing the words to make it flow better. He'd even used a dictionary to find out what 'substitutionary atonement' meant, but he still didn't understand it so he left it out. After the service, Harry came over to him and told him off for reading his prayer. Prayer, Harry told him, had to come 'straight from the heart'.

'But it did,' protested Tony. 'I meant every word of it.'

'Real prayer,' said Harry, 'doesn't need to be thought about. You just know what to say.'

You can understand why Tony didn't enjoy going to church. He actually thought that to be a Real Christian, you had to say Real Prayers and be just like Harry. Perhaps it would help if he attended the midweek meetings like Harry did, but it was terribly difficult. Apart from his family commitments, he used to collect money for 'Save the Children' and go to visit people who were in hospital and in prison. Those people liked him as he was, and didn't want him to be like Harry. What was he to do? He was sure that going to church was important, but he didn't like feeling so guilty all the time.

Tony couldn't understand why God was so concerned about the kind of prayers he used but not about the other things he thought were important. Didn't God care about the people he visited? Harry didn't seem to think so.

• He *shook his head*
• then he *shrugged his shoulders*
• then he *pointed his fingers* at Tony

'Shouldn't have got themselves sick or in trouble in the first place,' he said. Tony couldn't believe that that was how God really felt, but he knew that Real Christians didn't have doubts or ask difficult questions. Well, the only answer was that he wasn't a Real Christian and probably never would be. And that frightened him very much.

So on this particular Sunday, when Tony arrived at the church, he found a seat just inside the door, right at the back, and sat there. When they came to the 'Open Prayer Time', Tony was beginning to feel ill. Harry started his usual prayer. He thanked God for helping him to be a Real Christian. He said he could never have given four thousand pounds to the church if God hadn't strengthened him. And he thanked God for helping him say such wonderful prayers, and guaranteeing him a good place in heaven.

By the time Harry got to the end, Tony was feeling worse than he ever had before! Without thinking about it, he said, in an embarrassingly loud voice, 'God, forgive me for being such a terrible person!'

There was a deathly silence. No one else prayed aloud, and Tony just sat there, wondering what was going to happen at the end of the service. He didn't hear the sermon, and he couldn't bring himself to join in the hymns. He just sat there, thinking what a fool he had made of himself.

When the service ended, a group of people gathered around Tony. He thought he was in for a telling off for spoiling the service, but they all seemed to like him! They said it was the best prayer they had heard in their lives. 'Simple and to the point,' said one person. 'Absolutely sincere,' said another. Tony found that he had a lot of friends in the church, and that they actually thought very highly of him.

'Why d'you think you're so bad' asked Joan, who was a Pillar Of The Church. 'Everyone in the town loves you because of the way you help people.'

Tony noticed Harry standing all alone in a corner of the room and looking lonely. 'I'd better go and talk to him,' he thought.

The two men walked home together, and Harry seemed a lot quieter and less sure of himself than usual. 'Are you all right?' Tony asked.

'Oh, I'm all right,' said Harry. 'I just wish I could be a bit more like you.'

Our Story

Read out some of the prayers, or get the children themselves to do it if they're willing. Point out how few words were needed just to express what was felt. Then use some of the prayers as part of a prayer slot in the assembly.

Prayers

We're Sad

It's sad when religion is misused
to make people feel bad.
Please forgive us, God,
if ever we have done that.

We're Glad

It's wonderful to know you love us, God!
Thank you for finding so many ways
of showing us just how much you care,
and how important all people are to you.
Thank you for being so loving.

Let's Pray for People

We pray for all people who feel guilty,
or who feel pushed out of things
because of the way religion has been used.
Please, God, help us all to know that true
    religion
is about love and acceptance.
Help us to love and accept one another,
the way you love and accept us.

Songs

God doesn't want (SS)
I'm black, I'm white, I'm short, I'm tall (WUW)
Out to the great wide world we go! (WUW)
Thank you, O God, for all our friends (WW)
Stand up! Walk tall! (WW)
Sing a song of freedom (A)
When I needed a neighbour (CAP)
The best gift (CAP)
If I had a hammer (CAP)

Representation and Reality
God's Story

Narrator It was Sunday again, and Tony felt guilty. Everyone kept telling him that Christians should enjoy Sundays.

Tony *Real* Christians enjoy worship. What's wrong with me? I bet Harry Snooks will be there today, as usual.

Narrator Harry was a Real Christian: he was so good it hurt! Everyone knew how good Harry was, because Harry was always telling them. Every week, he was at the Prayer Meeting, the Bible Study and the 'Let's Spread the Gospel' Club – known among a few irreverents as Bible Bashers Anonymous.

Tony What I really dread is the Open Prayer slot in the service. One week, I spent most of Saturday writing a prayer out, and plucked up courage to use it on Sunday. Afterwards, Harry told me off for reading it.

Harry Real Prayer has to come straight from the heart.

Tony But it did. I worked really hard at getting it right.

Harry Real Prayer doesn't need to be thought about. You just know what to say.

Narrator Perhaps it would help if Tony attended the midweek meetings like Harry did, but it was terribly difficult. Apart from his family commitments, he used to collect money for 'Save the Children' and go to see people who were in prison – and he couldn't let all those people down. Tony had even begun to ask questions about how true it all was.

Tony If there's a God, why's he so concerned about the kind of prayers we use but not about the other things I'm doing? Doesn't God care about the prisoners?

Narrator
- Harry *shook his head*
- then he *shrugged his shoulders*
- then he *pointed his finger* at Tony

Harry	They shouldn't have got in trouble in the first place.
Narrator	When Tony arrived at the church this Sunday he found a seat just inside the door, right at the back. The service started and they sang some very jolly songs, but that just made Tony feel worse. Then they came to the 'Open Prayer Time', and Tony was feeling ill.
Harry	Thank you, God for helping me to be a Real Christian. I could never have given four thousand pounds to the church if you hadn't strengthened me. And I thank you for making me so good with words, so that I always say such great prayers. And thank you, God, for reserving me a good place in heaven.
Narrator	By the time Harry got to the end, Tony was feeling worse than ever. Suddenly he did an amazing thing.
Tony	*(Loudly)* God forgive me for being such a bad person!
Narrator	There was a deathly silence. Tony just sat there, thinking what a fool he had made of himself. When the service ended, a group of people gathered around him. Tony thought he was in for a telling off for spoiling the service, but they all seemed to like him!
Worshipper 1	What a wonderful prayer! Simple and to the point.
Worshipper 2	Absolutely sincere,
Narrator	Tony found that he had a lot of friends – including Joan, who was a Pillar Of The Church.
Joan	Why d'you think you're so bad? Everyone in the town loves you because of the way you help people.
Narrator	Tony couldn't believe it. Then he noticed Harry standing all alone in a corner of the room, and felt sorry for him. The two men walked home together, and Harry seemed a lot quieter and less sure of himself.
Tony	Are you all right?
Harry	Yes – but I just wish I could be a bit more like you.

Noncommittal Nick

Based on John 3:1-8

BEFORE THE DAY

Discuss with the children different kinds of choices. Some are easy to make and others more difficult. Get them to write down some examples, such as 'Cola or lemonade?' 'Biscuit or cake?' 'Wash up or wipe?' 'Chores or television?' Ask them if they sometimes have to choose between things that are difficult, because they either like or dislike both of them equally. Have those written down as well, and put up the choices on a display board.

• Think about the actions for all the children to join in during the story.

ON THE DAY

Introduction

Later on, we're going to think about making choices. First, we're going to say our 'Thank you' prayer.

'Thank you' Prayer

Thank you, God, for all you give us,
thank you for the earth and sea;
thank you, God, for special people,
thank you, God, for making me.

God's Story

There was a man called Nicodemus who was a member of the Jewish Council – a bit like being a Member or Parliament today. Well, Nicodemus was a real politician – he thought he could compromise his way through life with no problem. He prided himself on always being able to see both sides of a question, which is generally a good thing. What he couldn't understand, though, was that even if you see both sides, you sometimes have to make a choice. You can't go on for ever trying to face in two directions at once.

Nicodemus enjoyed going around the town in his fine councillor's clothes and seeing people smile at him and move out of his way. He liked the council meetings as well, when they used to discuss all kinds of things that they thought were terribly important, and use words that they thought no one else could understand. That really made them all feel superior.

Nicodemus knew about Jesus – and he and his friends on the Council were rather worried. What Jesus said seemed to make sense, and they had a sneaking feeling that Jesus was the special person God had promised to send to save the world. So they should have been pleased, but there was something they didn't like.

Jesus was going around saying that being rich and powerful wasn't important. He seemed to want everyone to care about poor people. Worse than that, he wanted them to share with nasty, dirty people – and with people who had horrible diseases that might be catching. Of course, Nicodemus felt sorry for those people, but he didn't think he could ever hug them the way Jesus did. Still, he was so impressed by Jesus that he decided to go and see him, and try and work out a compromise. 'I'd better go at night,' he thought. 'I don't want my friends knowing I've been to see Jesus.'

So late one evening, he sneaked along.

- He *looked to the left*
- and he *looked to the right*
- and he *beckoned with his finger*

Now Nicodemus was a politician – so he thought he knew how to get round people. 'Excuse me, Jesus,' he said, 'I do hope I'm not bothering you but you're such a good and clever person and you do the most wonderful, amazing, simply superfantapendous things . . .'

'Oh dear!' thought Jesus. 'A politician – you can always tell them.'

'If you want to follow me,' he said, 'it'll mean a complete change of life. Like being born all over again.'

'What?' said Nicodemus. 'I'm a bit big for that now, you know.'

'I'm telling you the truth,' Jesus said. 'You've got to change so much that you leave the old life behind – just like being born again. You can't go halfway and compromise on this one.'

Now I don't know about you, but I think Nicodemus understood exactly what Jesus was saying, but we've all done the same, haven't we? If we don't want to do what somebody's asking, it's easiest to say that we don't understand.

'Look, Nicodemus,' said Jesus, 'the world can offer you wonderful things: power, money, influence. But none of that lasts for ever – and neither does your life. Only God can give you the really important things – things that *do* last for ever. Go on, Nicodemus – let God change your life!'

'That sounds wonderful,' said Nicodemus. 'What do I have to do?'

'Just let go,' said Jesus. 'Stop trying to compromise and hang onto all the money and power. Stop worrying about what your friends will think. Let go of all that, and let God change your life.'

'Well, I'd like to of course,' said Nicodemus, 'but I've got a family, and a big house with a mortgage on it. And I'm a man of position. You can't expect me to give all that up.'

'That's the point,' said Jesus. 'Life with God is never clear-cut and easy. It's like the wind. You hear it blowing, but you never quite know where it's come from or where it's going. That's how it is with the life God gives.'

Nicodemus was unhappy. He really thought Jesus and his friends had a better kind of life than he did, for all his money and power. He could see that what Jesus was doing really meant something. And in his heart of hearts he really did care about the people Jesus helped. But he just couldn't bring himself to make a commitment. 'After all,' he thought, 'what's wrong with a bit of compromise? If I keep my money and my position, I can help those poor people – but it doesn't mean I've got to be one of them.'

So Nicodemus went sadly on his way. And Jesus stood there, just as sadly, and watched him go. After all, God doesn't want to force anybody to live his life – even though it would be wonderful if everyone did!

That wasn't the end of the story for Nicodemus. He carried on battling with himself for a long time before he finally made his choice.

Poor old Noncommittal Nick!

Our Story

Draw attention to the display. Have some fun with the groups asking them what they prefer, and at this stage make it a simple choice of one or other alternative. Then ask whether there were any of them that didn't put their hands up. Almost certainly there will have been – if not you can always use yourself as an example – because of course there is often a third choice of 'neither'. People who can't make up their minds generally end up with nothing.

Prayers

We're Sad

We're sorry, God,
for the times when we refuse
to commit ourselves
because we're afraid it might be difficult.
Give us the courage to do
what we believe to be right.

We're Glad

You're never noncommittal, God!
You always commit yourself to us,
and sometimes it causes you a lot of pain.
Thank you for always being committed.

Let's Pray for People

It's so easy to get trapped
by wealth, or by our own importance,
or by fear of what others might say.
We pray for people who would like
to be committed to you,
but are afraid of what they might lose.
Please help them to be brave.
And to make their choices.

Songs

God doesn't want (Appendix)
God is making a wonderful world (WUW)
Pick up your feet and go! (WUW)
Keep on travelling on! (WUW)
It's me, O Lord (A)
Love is his word (A)
Lord of the dance (CAP)
Give me oil in my lamp (CAP)
Morning has broken (CAP)

Noncommittal Nick
God's Story

Narrator There was a man called Nicodemus who was a member of the Jewish Council – a bit like being a Member of Parliament today. Like a lot of politicians, he thought he could talk his way through life with no problem. He prided himself on always seeing both sides of a question, which is good. What he couldn't understand, though, was that even if you see both sides, you sometimes have to make a choice. You can't go on for ever trying to face in two directions at once.

Nicodemus I'm very proud of being on the Council. I've got a lot of power, people respect me, and I enjoy the council meetings, when we discuss terribly important things.

Narrator Now at that time, Jesus was saying that being rich and powerful wasn't important. That worried Nicodemus, and he went to Jesus at night, so that his friends wouldn't see. He was very furtive.

- He *looked to the left*
- and he *looked to the right*
- and he *beckoned with his finger*

Nicodemus Excuse me, Jesus, I do hope I'm not bothering you but you're such a good person – and we know you must be God's messenger because you do the most wonderful, amazing, simply superfantapendous things . . .

Jesus Oh dear! A politician – you can always tell them. Look, if you want to follow me it'll mean a complete change of life. Like being born all over again.'

Nicodemus What?' I'm a bit big for that now you know.

Jesus It's the truth, You've got to leave the old life behind, just like being born again. You can't go halfway and compromise on this one.

Narrator	Now I think Nicodemus understood exactly what Jesus was saying, but he didn't like it, and so he played dumb.
Jesus	Look, Nicodemus, the world can offer you wonderful things: power, money, influence, but none of that lasts for ever. If you want the really important things, the world can't give you those. Only God can. That's why you can't compromise. Go on, Nicodemus – let God change your life!
Nicodemus	That sounds wonderful. What do I have to do?
Jesus	Just let go. Stop trying to compromise and hang onto all the money and power. Stop worrying about what your friends will think or whether you'll be able to afford nice clothes. Let go of all that, and let God change your life.
Nicodemus	Well, I'd like to of course, but it's not that simple. I've got a family, and a big house. And I'm someone who's respected in the neighbourhood. You can't expect me to give all that up.
Jesus	That's the point. Life with God is never clear-cut and easy. It's like the wind. You hear it blowing, but you never quite know where it's come from or where it's going. That's how it is with the life God gives.
Narrator	Nicodemus was unhappy. He really thought Jesus and his friends had a better kind of life than he did, for all his money and power. He could see that what Jesus was doing really meant something. And in his heart of hearts he really did care about the people Jesus helped. But he just couldn't bring himself to make a commitment.
Nicodemus	After all, what's wrong with a bit of compromise? If I keep my money and my position, I can help those poor people – but it doesn't mean I've got to be one of them.
Narrator	So Nicodemus went sadly on his way. And Jesus stood there, just as sadly, and watched him go. After all, God doesn't want to force anybody to live his life – even though it would be wonderful if everyone did! That wasn't the end of the story for Nicodemus. He carried on battling with himself for a long time before he finally made his choice. Poor old Noncommittal Nick!

Wait for the Power

Based on Acts 2:1-21

BEFORE THE DAY

What do the children think they might be when they grow up? Write a list of examples, and/or get the children to draw themselves as they expect to be when they are older.

- Think about the actions for all the children to join in during the story.

ON THE DAY

Introduction

This morning, we're going to learn about waiting, but first, we'll say our 'Thank you' prayer.

'Thank you' Prayer

Thank you, God, for all you give us,
thank you for the earth and sea;
thank you, God, for special people,
thank you, God, for making me.

God's Story

The friends of Jesus were waiting, all together, in a secret meeting room. When Jesus had gone back to heaven, he had said, 'Stay in Jerusalem until you get the power you need.' Peter was getting impatient, though. 'It's all very well,' he said, 'but the city is full of people. We should be telling people about Jesus.'

'Jesus told us to wait,' said Matthew, who used to be a tax collector before he met Jesus. 'I know all about waiting – people used to keep me waiting for months.'

'It's no good, anyway,' added James. 'The visitors are from all over the world – we'd need to know dozens of different languages if we were going to tell them about Jesus.'

'Let's be honest,' said Thomas. 'We don't really want to go out there. There are people who want to kill us, and I'm too young to die – come to think of it, I always will be.'

As usual, Thomas was the most honest one of the group; he was saying what the others were afraid to say. In their hearts, everybody knew that he was right. That was why they'd bolted the doors and not told anyone else where they were. The friends of Jesus were good people, and good friends – but they had reason to be afraid; the people who had killed Jesus were now looking for his followers, and they weren't going to invite them to tea! Most people would be just as frightened as they were if they had to face that kind of thing.

The problem was, though, how were they ever going to get the courage to do Jesus' work? They had seen him several times after he had risen from the dead, and yet they still seemed to be frightened of being killed themselves. How could that ever be changed? No wonder they were a little bit glum!

Just as they were beginning to get desperate, and thinking what dreadful, useless disciples they were, they heard a strange sound. 'Close the window, Andrew,' said John. 'Sounds like the wind's getting up.'

'It's already closed,' said Andrew. 'We barred it up to keep the religious leaders out so that they can't hurt us.'

'Well you didn't do it properly,' grumbled Peter. 'That's the trouble with you – you can't be trusted.'

'Ooh! Look who's talking!' Andrew responded, and he would have said a lot more but Thomas stopped him. He didn't think it was the wind at all.

- He *licked his finger*
- and he *held it up in the air*
- and he *shook his head*

He couldn't feel any draught at all.

And all the disciples sat very quietly and listened. Sure enough, the noise got louder and louder, but they couldn't feel the wind. Thomas was just thinking that it was a bit like the burning bush – when Moses had seen the flames, but the bush didn't actually burn – when he noticed flames as well.

'Hey, Peter!' he said. 'Your hair's on fire!'

'Don't be daft!' said Peter, 'I'd know if *my* hair was on fire. You're the one who's got that problem.'

Then they realised that there seemed to be flames over everybody's head. 'It *is* like the burning bush!' thought Thomas. 'Something special's happening.'

'Come on!' shouted Peter. 'Let's go outside and . . .' But he was too late. They'd gone. They'd unbolted the door and gone rushing out into the street and started telling everyone that Jesus was alive – and all of a sudden they were language experts! Andrew was speaking in Persian to a group of carpet merchants, while Philip had cornered a couple of soldiers and was talking in Latin, and Thomas – who had always doubted the importance of learning languages – was busy winning an argument with some philosophers, in Greek.

Then Peter realised what he was doing. 'This is silly,' he thought. 'We could get ourselves into serious trouble doing this.' He realised he was still quite frightened, but then he thought, 'Well some things are worth getting into trouble for – and there's nothing more important than doing this.'

That morning, thousands of people heard the good news that Jesus was alive. The religious authorities didn't like it. 'What will happen to all our power and our privileges,' they asked, 'if ordinary people start being listened to?' So they went around saying that Peter and his friends were drunk.

'Do me a favour!' laughed Peter. 'At this time of the morning? This is the power of God at work, but you're too bothered about yourselves to recognise it.'

Then the disciples realised that this was the 'power' Jesus had promised them. They knew there would still be hard and dangerous times ahead, because Jesus had told them that, too. But they knew it was worth it. Now they understood that, whatever happened, Jesus would always be with them and God wouldn't let their lives or their work be wasted.

Now that's what I call power!

Our Story

Point out the display which your class prepared and describe a few of the ambitions. 'Stephanie wants to be an airline pilot', or whatever. Then ask why they can't be those things now, and the answers may be many and varied but will probably amount to the fact that they are not yet ready. In just the same way, the disciples were not ready for what they had to do. Sometimes, waiting in patience can be very hard!

Prayers

We're Sad

Sometimes it's difficult to understand
people who are different from us,
but that's no reason not to try.
Please, God, forgive us
for letting differences keep us apart.

We're Glad

Holy Spirit,
you break down all the barriers
between different people.
Thank you for making it possible
for us to listen to one another.

Let's Pray for People

We pray for the world,
full of many different kinds of people,
speaking different languages,
and even using the same words differently.
Please, God, give us the gift of understanding,
and stop us being afraid of each other.

Songs

I'm black, I'm white, I'm short, I'm tall (WUW)
God is making a wonderful world (WUW)
Out to the great wide world we go! (WUW)
Peace is flowing like a river (A)
Give me oil in my lamp (CAP)
One more step (CAP)
Spirit of God (CAP)
The family of man (CAP)

Wait for the Power
God's Story

Narrator	Jesus had gone back to heaven, leaving his friends to carry on his work. He'd told them not to start straight away but to stay in Jerusalem until he gave them the power they needed. Peter was getting impatient.
Peter	It's all very well, Matthew, but the city is full of people. We shan't have another chance like this for nearly a year. We should be telling people about Jesus.
Matthew	Jesus told us to wait. I know all about waiting – when I was a tax man, people kept me waiting for months. Anyway, we'd need to know dozens of different languages – wouldn't we, Thomas?
Thomas	Let's be honest. We don't really want to go out there, anyway. There are people who want to kill us, and I'm too young to die – come to think of it, I always will be.
Narrator	As usual, Thomas was the most honest one of the group. In their hearts, everybody knew that he was right. That was why they'd bolted themselves in.
Peter	Close the window, Andrew. Sounds like the wind's getting up.
Andrew	It's already closed. We nailed it up for security.
Peter	Well you didn't do it properly.
Narrator	Thomas didn't think it was the wind, anyway.

- He *licked his finger*
- and he *held it up in the air*
- and he *shook his head*

Thomas	It's not the wind. I can't feel any draught at all.

Narrator	All the disciples sat very quietly and listened. The noise got louder, but the air was still.
Thomas	Hey, Peter! Your hair's on fire!
Peter	Don't be daft! I'd know if my hair was on fire. You're the one who's got that problem.
Narrator	Then they realised that there seemed to be flames over everybody's head. Suddenly, they unbolted the door and went rushing out into the street and started telling everyone that Jesus was alive – and all of a sudden they were language experts! Andrew was speaking in Persian to a group of carpet merchants, while Philip had cornered a couple of soldiers and was talking in Latin, and Thomas – who had always doubted the importance of learning languages – was busy winning an argument with some philosophers, in Greek.
Peter	This is silly. We could get ourselves into serious trouble doing this. Still, some things are worth getting into trouble for – and this is important.
Narrator	That morning, thousands of people heard the good news that Jesus was alive. The religious authorities didn't like it because they were afraid of losing their power. So they went around saying that Peter and his friends were drunk.
Peter	Do me a favour! At this time of the morning? This is the power of God at work, but you're too bothered about yourselves to recognise it.
Narrator	Then the disciples realised that this was the 'power' Jesus had promised them. They knew there would still be hard and dangerous times ahead because Jesus had told them that, too. But they knew it was worth it. Now they understood that, whatever happened, Jesus would always be with them and God wouldn't let their lives or their work be wasted. Now that's what I call power!

A Disciple in the Desert

Based on Acts 8:26-39

BEFORE THE DAY

Children are very good at making friends on holiday. Get them to talk about people they have met, and either write or draw about them. Make a display of the work.

- Think about the actions for all the children to join in during the story.

ON THE DAY

Introduction

Our story today will be about a very special meeting between two strangers. First, we're going to say our 'Thank you' prayer.

'Thank you' Prayer

Thank you, God, for all you give us,
thank you for the earth and sea;
thank you, God, for special people,
thank you, God, for making me.

God's Story

Jim was a very important man; he was chief adviser to the queen of Ethiopia. This was partly because Jim knew an awful lot about the rest of the world. He understood the customs and religious beliefs of other countries, and he could always see things from other people's point of view – and that's something that all really important people ought to be able to do.

One day, Jim went to the queen and said, 'I'd like to go to the Jerusalem festival this year, Your Majesty, if you could give me some time off.'

The queen let him go, but she sent a servant with him to make sure he was well looked after and said, 'Don't stay too long – I might need you here.'

Jim had a wonderful time at the festival, even though he had to go home while the celebrations were still in full swing. Before he set out, though, he went to buy himself a souvenir.

Meanwhile, also in Jerusalem was Philip, who was one of Jesus' friends. Jesus had gone back to heaven a few weeks before, but his friends knew that he was still with them, although they couldn't see him. Philip was wondering whether there was anything particular that Jesus wanted him to do, when he had a strange idea that he ought to go for a walk along the Gaza Road. Now Gaza Road went through the desert and that was not a good place to be. Philip thought it would be much nicer to stay in Jerusalem where there was good company, plenty of food and drink, and parties going on all the time. There again, one can have too much of the parties and perhaps the walk and a bit of quiet would do him good. So he told his brother Andrew where he was going and set off toward Gaza.

At about the time Philip left, Jim was still looking for his souvenir. What about a nice piece of Jerusalem Rock? But Jerusalem Rock is not the same as Blackpool Rock!

- He *licked it*
- then he tried to *bite a piece off*
- and then he *pulled a horrible face*

'Ugh!' he said. 'This may be fine for building temples on, but you can't eat it.' He'd always thought that chariot stickers saying 'I've been to Jerusalem' were rather silly, so he looked around for something more special. 'I know,' he thought. 'I'll buy myself a bible. It will remind me of my visit, and I'll have something to read on the journey home.' So he bought his bible and went back to where his servant was keeping an eye on the chariot. 'That's it,' he said. 'We can go home now. You drive, Josh, and I'll have a read.'

As it happened, Jim opened his bible at a story called *The Suffering Servant*. He felt sorry for this servant who seemed to be having a very hard time, but he was also puzzled. 'Who is this person?' he thought.

Just as they got out into the desert, Josh called out, 'There's some chap walking on the road. D'you think he's lost?' Jim was going to say, 'Stop and see if we can help,' when the man turned and walked towards them.

'Good morning!' said Philip. 'Are you enjoying your book?'

'Yes, very much,' replied Jim, 'but I don't really understand it.'

'I think I can probably explain it to you,' said Philip.

'Oh, that's wonderful!' said Jim. 'If you're going my way, why not hop in?'

Philip got into the chariot and Josh started driving again. 'What I want to know,' said Jim, 'is whether this writer is writing about himself or somebody else.'

'It's a prophecy,' said Philip, 'and it's only recently come true. It's about Jesus who loved people so much that he died for them.' Then Philip went on and told Jim all about his friend Jesus who had died, risen again and gone back to heaven, but had promised always to be with them.

Jim thought it was a wonderful story. 'How do I become a friend of Jesus, like you?' he asked.

'Be baptised,' said Philip. 'It's a sign that you want to make a new start – like being washed clean.'

'Well,' said Jim, 'here's an oasis, so you can baptise me now.' Josh thought they must have gone mad, but he didn't say anything – after all, even friends of Jesus could lose their tempers, and Jim was a powerful man!

Philip was wondering what he should do next, because he had travelled a long way in the chariot and although he liked walking he didn't fancy that long a walk – especially in the midday sun. Jim had thought of that, and was going to offer to run Philip back, but suddenly Philip wasn't there any more. God had whisked him off somewhere else – after all, there were still lots of other people who wanted to hear about Jesus.

Jim carried on toward Ethiopia. On the way he read the story of *The Suffering Servant* again. He found it had a whole new meaning because of what he'd been told about Jesus. When he arrived back, the queen was very pleased to see him.

'Did you have a good time in Jerusalem?' she asked.

'Oh yes, thank you, Your Majesty,' answered Jim, 'but the really exciting part happened on the way back.'

Our Story

Look at the display and describe some of the contributions to the wider group of children. Have they other stories to contribute? It always pays to keep alert when you're in a strange place. You meet the most interesting people!

Prayers

We're Sad

Sometimes, God, you ask us
to go to places we'd rather not.
Please forgive us for the times
when we have been unwilling to go.

We're Glad

We want to say thank you, God,
for people who have gone out of their way
in order to help us.
Thank you for caring about us
and thank you for such loving people.

Let's Pray for People

We pray for people who are puzzled;
who can't quite work out what it is
that you are saying to them.
Please send people to them
who can help them to understand,
and make us all willing
to help one another.

Songs

Questions! Questions! (SS)
I'm black, I'm white, I'm short, I'm tall (WUW)
Jesus had all kinds of friends (WUW)
Out to the great wide world we go! (WUW)
Keep on travelling on (WUW)
When I needed a neighbour (CAP)
The family of man (CAP)
Black and white (CAP)
The best gift (CAP)

A Disciple in the Desert
God's Story

Narrator Philip, who was one of Jesus' friends, was in Jerusalem for the annual festival. Jesus had gone back to heaven a few weeks before, but his friends knew that he was still with them although they couldn't see him. So Philip was wondering whether there was anything particular that Jesus wanted him to do.

Philip I think I'll go for a walk. All the celebrations are getting a bit heavy and I fancy somewhere quiet. So if anyone wants me I'll be along the Gaza Road.

Narrator Also in Jerusalem was Jim. He was the chief adviser to the queen of Ethiopia. He had come to Jerusalem for the festival, but now it was time to go home. Before he set out, though, there was one more thing he had to do: buy himself a souvenir, such as a nice piece of Jerusalem Rock. But Jerusalem Rock is not the same as Blackpool Rock!

- He *licked it*
- then he tried to *bite a piece off*
- and then he *pulled a horrible face*

Jim Ugh! This may be fine for building temples on, but you can't eat it. And I'm not mad about silly chariot stickers saying 'I've been to Jerusalem', either. I know – I'll buy myself a bible. It will remind me of my visit, and I'll have something to read on the journey home.

Narrator So he bought his bible and went back to where his servant was keeping an eye on the chariot.

Jim That's it, we can go home now. You drive, Josh, and I'll have a read.

Narrator	As it happened, Jim opened his bible at a story called *The Suffering Servant.* He felt very sorry for this servant who seemed to be having a terribly hard time, but he was also puzzled, wondering who the person could be. What Jim needed was someone to explain it to him. Just then, Josh noticed something.
Josh	There's some chap walking on the road. D'you think he's lost?
Jim	Stop and see if we can help. Oh, he's coming over.
Philip	Good morning! Are you enjoying your book?
Jim	Yes, very much, but I don't really understand it.
Philip	I think I can probably explain it to you.
Jim	Oh, that's wonderful! Can I give you a lift?
Narrator	Philip got into the chariot and Josh started driving again while Philip and Jim read together.
Jim	What I want to know is whether this writer is writing about himself or somebody else.
Philip	It's a prophecy that's only recently come true, about Jesus who loved people so much that he died for them.
Narrator	Then Philip went on and told Jim all about his friend Jesus who had died, risen again and gone back to heaven, but had promised always to be with them.
Jim	How do I become a friend of Jesus, like you?
Philip	Be baptised. It's a sign that you want to make a new start – like being washed clean.
Jim	Well, here's an oasis, so you can baptise me now.
Narrator	After Philip had baptised Jim, he was just wondering what he should do next when God whisked him off somewhere else. There were still lots of other people who wanted to hear about Jesus.

God Has No Favourites

Based on Acts 10

BEFORE THE DAY

What kinds of food do the children eat? Get them to bring in empty packets or labels from their and their families' favourites. Alternatively, they can draw and colour them.

• Think about the actions for all the children to join in during the story.

ON THE DAY

Introduction

It's a good thing we're not all the same in this world. Before we think about that a little more, let's say our 'Thank you' prayer.

'Thank you' Prayer

Thank you, God, for all you give us,
thank you for the earth and sea;
thank you, God, for special people,
thank you, God, for making me.

God's Story

Cornelius was an officer in the Roman army. Although he had a lot of Jewish friends, he was not allowed into their houses and they couldn't go into his. That was because of the laws they had to observe.

One day, Cornelius had a visit from an angel. At first, he was frightened.

'Don't worry,' said the angel. 'God's sent me to say how pleased he is with you.'

'Well, bless me!' said Cornelius.

'Give me time,' said the angel. 'I was just coming to that. You've got to get in touch with a man called Peter, at Joppa. He's lodging near the sea front with a leather worker called Simon. Ask Peter to come over and see you.'

Cornelius called his servant. 'Antonio,' he said, 'I've got a job for you.'

'Oh, dear, sir!' exclaimed Antonio. 'You haven't got blood on your best tunic again, have you? I do wish you'd be more careful Remember what I've told you: it's off-the-peg battledress for the horrible, gory jobs, and made to measure tunic and kilt for ceremonial parades only.'

'No, don't worry, Antonio – it's not that,' said Cornelius with a smile. 'I want you to go and look for a leatherworker.'

'Look for a leatherworker, eh?' mused Antonio. 'Obviously a case of "hide and seek". Get it? "Hide" and seek – you see sir, "hide" is another name for – oh, never mind. Where is this leatherworker, then?'

'He's in Joppa,' explained Cornelius. 'He lives right by the sea front.'

'Oh, does he!' returned Antonio. 'So I suppose when he goes home he goes "back to front"! No? Back to front? A pun, you see, sir – when he goes back, he – Oh what's the use!'

'Quite!' said Cornelius. 'Now I want you to ask for a man called Peter.'

'That sounds Okay,' said Antonio. 'I'll just knock an the door and say . . .'

'I think the sooner you leave the better, don't you?' Cornelius interrupted him, and Antonio left, muttering to himself.

• He *pulled on his boots*
• and he *buttoned up his coat*
• and he *rode off on his horse*

Meanwhile, in Joppa, Peter was on the flat roof of Simon's house praying. He was hungry, and just as he was wondering whether dinner was ready yet he had an amazing vision. He saw a great big sailcloth coming down out of the sky, as though it was held by the four corners. When it got low enough, he peeped over the side of it and saw lots and lots of different animals.

'There you are, Peter,' said God. 'Eat one of those.'

'I can't do that!' exclaimed Peter. 'Those are dirty animals – you know I can only eat the food which our religion counts as clean.'

'It's what I say that matters,' said God, 'and if I say something's clean, who are you to disagree?'

Altogether, this happened three times.

Then, there was a knock at the door; and when Simon opened it Peter heard a voice say, 'Hello, I'm Antonio. You probably know my twin brother – supplier of office equipment to the emperor. No? Well, never mind. I've come to see Peter. Can I see him, or is Peter out? Tee hee hee! Get it? "Peter out"?

'Hey, Peter!' called Simon. 'There's a comedian here to see you.'

'Oh, no!' thought Peter. Then he had an idea. 'Tell him he can't come in,' he called to Simon. 'He's a foreigner and he's not ritually pure.'

'I heard that,' Antonio shouted back. 'I'm as pure as you are. Anyway, it was your God who told my boss to send for you so don't you come all that purity malarkey with me.'

Then Peter remembered what God had said in his vision: 'If I say something's clean, who are you to disagree?'

Well, to cut a long story short – and spare you any more of Antonio's horrible jokes – Peter let Antonio stay the night, and then went with him to where Cornelius lived. He told Cornelius all about Jesus: about how the powerful people had killed him and how he'd risen from the dead. Cornelius looked a bit embarrassed at that, but Peter told him not to worry. 'It's the future that matters,' he said. 'You can't change the past, but you can help transform the future. That's what resurrection's about'

So Cornelius was baptised, and became a follower of Jesus, and Antonio did too.

'I've learnt a lot today,' said Peter. 'God really doesn't have any favourites – he loves everybody just as much.'

'That's wonderful,' said Cornelius, looking relieved. 'Does that mean he'll fix things so that I don't have to put up with Antonio telling me those dreadful jokes?'

'No,' said Peter. 'I'm afraid not.'

Our Story

Show the children the display which the class have made and ask for other contributions of favourite foods. There should be quite a variety. God used the variety of food available to teach Peter not to be fussy about *people*.

Prayers

We're Sad

We're sorry, God, for wanting
to be your favourites.
Help us to remember that you love
everyone just as much.

We're Glad

Thank you, loving God,
for not having favourites.
Thank you for loving us all
even when we don't deserve it.
Thank you for always being here
and never leaving us on our own.

Let's Pray for People

Caring God,
There are people who think that
you don't love them.
This makes them very unhappy.
Please help us to show them
that you love them just as much
as you love other people.

Songs

God doesn't want (SS)
I'm black, I'm white, I'm short, I'm tall (WUW)
Jesus had all kinds of friends (WUW)
Stand up! Walk tall! (WW)
It's me, O Lord (A)
The family of man (CAP)
He's got the whole world in his hand (CAP)
Black and white (CAP)

God Has No Favourites
God's Story

Narrator Cornelius was a Roman officer. He had a lot of Jewish friends, but he was sad that they weren't allowed to visit him. One day, an angel came to see him.

Angel God's sent me to say how pleased he is with you.

Cornelius Well, bless me!

Angel Give me time, I was just coming to that. You're to send for a man called Peter, who's staying at Joppa. He's lodging near the sea front with a leather worker called Simon.

Cornelius Antonio, I've got a job for you.

Antonio Oh, dear, Sir! You haven't got blood on your best tunic again, have you? I do wish you'd be more careful. It's off-the-peg battledress for the horrible, gory jobs, and made to measure tunic and kilt for parades only.

Cornelius No, don't worry, Antonio – it's not that. I want you to go and look for a leatherworker.

Antonio Obviously a case of 'hide and seek'. Get it? You see sir, 'hide' is another name for – oh, never mind.

Cornelius Quite. He's in Joppa. He lives right by the sea front.

Antonio I suppose when he goes home he goes 'back to front'! A pun, you see, sir – when he – Oh what's the use!

Cornelius I want you to ask for a man called Peter.

Antonio That sounds okay. I'll just knock an the door and say . . .

Cornelius I think the sooner you leave the better, don't you?

Antonio (*Aside*) Not much to ask, is it? Just to work for a master with a sense of humour, who knows his ceremonial uniform from his battle fatigues – that's all!

Narrator	Antonio did as he was told.

- He *pulled on his boots*
- and he *buttoned up his coat*
- and he *rode off on his horse*

	Meanwhile, Peter was on the flat roof of Simon's house praying. He was hungry, and had an amazing vision. He saw a great sailcloth coming out of the sky, and in it were lots and lots of different animals. Then God spoke to him.
God	There you are, Peter. Eat one of those.
Peter	You know I can only eat ritually clean food!
God	If I say something's clean, who are you to disagree?
Narrator	This happened three times, and while Peter was wondering what it meant, he heard a voice at the door.
Antonio	Hello, I've come to see Peter. Can I see him, or is Peter out? Tee hee hee! Get it? Oh, please yourself!
Peter	Oh, no! Not an amateur comedian. Tell him he can't come in – he's a foreigner and he's not ritually pure.
Antonio	I heard that. It was your God who told my boss to send for you so don't come that purity malarkey with me.
Narrator	Then Peter remembered what God had said.
God	If I say something's clean, who are you to disagree?'
Narrator	Peter went to see Cornelius. Cornelius was baptised, and became a follower of Jesus, and Antonio did too.
Peter	I've learnt a lot today. God really does love everyone, with no favourites.
Cornelius	Does that mean he'll fix things so that I don't have to put up with Antonio telling me those dreadful jokes?
Peter	No, I'm afraid not.

The Angel, the Apostle and the Great Escape

Based on Acts 12:1-19

BEFORE THE DAY

Have a fun session with the children. Ask them which famous people they would like to have locked up – and why. It could be the weather forecaster who got it wrong on their day out, or the star of a 'soap' which rivals their favourite, or perhaps the key player in a rival football club . . . Cut out some pictures from newspapers, etc. and put them on display. You could also make some 'bars' out of black tape and pin those across the pictures. Be careful to point out that this is only a game, and it's not funny when it really happens to people.

• Think about the actions for all the children to join in during the story.

ON THE DAY

Introduction

In a few minutes we're going to put some famous people in prison. First, we'll say our 'Thank you' prayer.

'Thank you' Prayer

Thank you, God, for all you give us,
thank you for the earth and sea;
thank you, God, for special people,
thank you, God, for making me.

God's Story

King Herod Agrippa was a rather unpleasant character. He was terribly unpopular, and so he did what politicians always do then – he looked for easy ways of making people like him.

Now at that time, the Christians were almost as unpopular as Herod was, which gave Herod an idea. He had James, who had been one of the really close friends of Jesus, arrested and cut his head off. The mob liked that very much indeed, so Herod had Peter arrested, too.

One night, Peter was sleeping, chained up between two guards with the others keeping watch outside, when he felt a tap on his shoulder. The cell was full of light, and there was an angel standing beside him. Well, he *thought* it was an angel – or was it?

'Hi there, Peter baby!' said the angel 'Hey, what are you waiting for? Come with me – and look lively now, I haven't got all night.'

Peter thought this must be a dream. Well, wouldn't you? 'You don't talk like an angel,' he said.

'Takes all kinds to make a heaven, baby!' said the angel. 'Now are you coming? I've left a party that's out of this world to come and get you out, so show a leg. Put your coat on, though, 'cos baby, it's cold outside. Now walk this way, son.' With that, the angel led the way. He seemed to be hearing music.

- He *snapped his fingers*
- and he *nodded his head*
- and he *swayed from side to side*

Now Peter was *sure* he was dreaming. 'If I could walk that way,' he thought, 'I'd be in show business.' Then he realised his chains had fallen off and he could move around. So he put his coat on and followed the angel out of the prison, past the guards who looked straight through them without seeing, and into the city. The angel was setting a cracking pace, and every so often, he would look round and say, 'C'm on, Peter baby – get with that crazy beat!'

Peter was really hoping that the dream wouldn't end too soon when the angel said, 'That's it, Buddy Boy. Gotta get back. Woweeeee what a party!' And with that, he was gone, leaving Peter standing in the middle of the road on his own.

The night was cold, just as the angel had said, and so Peter make his way to the house where Mary lived – no, not that Mary, there were Marys everywhere in those days. This Mary lived with her son, John Mark. Peter knocked on the door, and one of the maids, called Rhoda, came to see who it was.

'Ello! 'Oo is it?' she called through the door.

'It's me. Peter.'

'Go on!' answered Rhoda. 'You're 'avin' me on – Peter's in prison, Peter is.'

'Oh, come on, Rhoda – it's cold out here!' said Peter.

Then Rhoda recognised Peter's voice. 'Ooh it is!' she shouted. 'It's 'im! 'Ere, missis – you'll never guess 'oo's outside!' And she went running back into the living room, leaving Peter still standing outside in the cold. 'Oh, do be quiet, Rhoda,' said Mary. 'That's a very bad joke.'

'No, honest, it's 'im.' Said Rhoda 'I allus know Peter's voice, 'cos 'e talks funny.'

Meanwhile, Peter was getting impatient. 'Hey!' he called out. 'It's me you silly girl – open the door.'

Well, you should have seen Mary's face when she found it really was Peter. Mind you, that was nothing compared with Herod's face when he discovered that Peter was gone. 'I don't believe it!' he screamed. 'Four of you, armed to the teeth, to guard one lousy prisoner who's chained and locked in a cell, and you can't even do that.'

'We're very sorry, Your Majesty,' said the chief guard. 'We just don't know what happened to him.'

'"Don't know"? "Don't know"?' screeched Herod. 'It's your perishing job to know. More to the point, it's your job not to let it happen. Now what am I going to do? I promised the people a nice juicy beheading. Well, someone's got to lose their noddle, and since you can't use yours you won't miss them will you.'

That's what power can do to people, you see. They get everything out of proportion, and start behaving irrationally. And in the end it didn't do Herod any good: all the power in the world wouldn't stop him from dying a horrible death.

It makes you think, doesn't it: there must be a better way of doing things.

Our Story

Show the assembly the display and ask why those people are in prison. The answers will probably be that someone is afraid of them or angry with them, or that it is to someone else's advantage that they are there. But those aren't good reasons for doing it to them, are they? You see, Herod wasn't so unusual, was he?

Prayers

We're Sad

Please forgive us, God,
if we've been unfair to people;
if we've blamed someone for something
without being sure it was their fault,
or let them take the blame
for something we have done.

We're Glad

Thank you, God, for caring,
and for setting people free.
Thank you for loving us, even when
we're not very loving to others.

Let's Pray for People

Lots of people need to be set free.
We all need to be freed from our own prejudice,
or from being addicted to money or power.
Please God, send your angel
and set us all free!

Songs

Get with the beat (SS)
Out to the great wide world we go! (WUW)
Break out (CAP)
If I had a hammer (CAP)
You shall go out with joy (CAP)

The Angel, the Apostle and the Great Escape
God's Story

Narrator King Herod Agrippa was a rather unpleasant character who seemed to come from a long line of similar nasties. He was terribly unpopular, and so he did what politicians always do – he looked for easy ways of making people like him.

Herod Let me see – a good execution's the thing. The people loved it when I killed that Christian fellow, James. Of course! I can get rid of Christians and make myself more popular both at the same time.

Narrator So he had Peter arrested and used sixteen guards working in four shifts to keep watch on him. One night, Peter was sleeping between two guards with the others keeping watch outside, when he felt a tap on his shoulder. The cell was full of light, and there was an angel standing beside him. Well, he *thought* it was an angel – or was it?

Angel Hi there, Peter baby! Hey, what are you waiting for? Come along, look lively now, I haven't got all night.

Narrator Peter thought it must be a dream. Well, wouldn't you?

Peter You don't talk like an angel.

Angel Takes all kinds to make a heaven, baby! Now are you coming? I've left a party that's out of this world to come and get you out, so show a leg. Put your coat on, though, 'cos baby, it's cold outside. Now walk this way, son.

Narrator With that, the angel led the way. He seemed to be hearing music.

- He *snapped his fingers*
- and he *nodded his head*
- and he *swayed from side to side*

	Peter thought he might as well enjoy the dream. So he followed the angel out of the prison, past the guards and into the city. The angel was setting a cracking pace.
Angel	C'm on, Peter baby – get with that crazy beat!
Narrator	Peter really hoped the dream wouldn't end too soon.
Angel	That's it, Buddy Boy. Gotta go. Wow-ee what a party!
Peter	It's true. God sent an angel to help me. Well, I think it was an angel . . . Yes, of course, Jesus always uses the last people you'd expect. It was an angel!
Narrator	Peter went to the house where Mary lived – no, not that Mary, there were Marys everywhere in those days – with her son, John Mark. Peter knocked on the door, and a maid called Rhoda came to see who it was.
Rhoda	Ello! 'Oo is it?
Peter	It's me. Peter.
Rhoda	Go on! You're 'avin' me on – Peter's in prison, Peter is.
Peter	Oh, come on, Rhoda – it's cold out here!
Rhoda	Ooh it is! It's 'im! 'Ere, missis – Peter's outside!
Mary	Oh, do be quiet, Rhoda. That's a very bad joke.
Rhoda	Honest! I allus know Peter's voice, 'cos 'e talks funny.
Peter	Hey! Rhoda! It's me you silly girl – open the door.
Narrator	Well, you should have seen Mary's face when she came to the door and found it really was Peter. Mind you, that was nothing compared with Herod's face when he discovered that Peter was gone. I'd have loved to have seen it – wouldn't you?

Songs

Get With The Beat

To the tune of *Little Brown Jug*

The prison cell was locked and barred
with a couple of heavies standing guard,
'till an angel came along
and woke the captive with his song.

Refrain:
'Ha, ha, ha! Hee, hee, hee!
Baby I'm gonna set you free!
Ha, ha, ha! Hee, hee, hee!
Get with the beat and follow me!'

The angel then went on to say,
'Put a spring in your step and walk this way!
See, the doors are open wide,
and all the guards are glassy-eyed!'

Refrain:

'Oh Peter, Baby, move those feet,
will you get on that crazy freedom beat!
Ain't got time to hesitate,
we're gonna dance and celebrate!'

Refrain:

Now all around the world today
there are people unfairly locked away.
We can join the angel's song
and move that freedom beat along.

Refrain:

Jesus Can Make Us Truly Rich

To the tune of *Here we go round the Mulberry bush*

Jesus can make us truly rich,
truly rich,
truly rich.
Jesus can make us truly rich
when he helps us love each other.

Let it Be!

To the tune of *Three Blind Mice*

'Let it be!
Let it be!'
That's what he said.
That's what he said.
The universe was a dreadful sight
a terrible mess and as dark as night,
then God spoke the word and said, 'Let there be light,
O let it be!'

'Let it be!
Let it be!'
That's what he said.
That's what he said.
'Let's get things sorted without delay,
the earth from the sky and the night from day,
now that's looking better, I'm happy to say,
so let it be!'

'Let it be!
Let it be!'
That's what he said.
That's what he said.
'I'm separating the earth and sea,
the land will be covered in flow'rs and trees,
now that's looking pretty delightful to me,
so let it be!'

'Let it be!
Let it be!'
That's what he said.
That's what he said.
'Let's fill creation with life diverse,
let earth be a gem in the universe,
and now I'll make people for better or worse,
so let it be!'

Rabbles, Babbles

To the tune of *Baa, Baa, Black Sheep*

Rabbles, babbles, what's it all about?
people talk and people shout.
Nobody listens, so no one is heard,
for everyone's trying hard to have the last word!

Rabbles, babbles echo all around;
empty vessels make most sound!
Sometimes, to listen in silence is best,
to switch off our wagging tongues and give them a rest.

Questions! Questions!

To the tune of *Twinkle, Twinkle, Little Star*

Questions! Questions! What a lot!
'Who', 'Why', 'Where,' 'How', 'When' and What'!
They're the tools for finding out
what the world is all about.
Questions! Questions! What a lot!
'Who', 'Why', 'Where,' 'How', 'When' and What'!

Questions! Questions! What a lot!
'Who', 'Why',' 'Where,' 'How', 'When' and What'!
Keep on asking, never fear,
they're what grown-ups love to hear![3]
Questions! Questions! What a lot!
'Who', 'Why', 'Where,' 'How', 'When' and What'!

---

[3] Okay, so put your tongue in your cheek, or cross your fingers or something!

Be Yourself!

To the tune of *Three Blind Mice*

Be yourself!
Be yourself!
That's all you need!
That's all you need!
You needn't pose as a superstar,
or say that a Porsche is your other car,
for better or worse, you're the person you are,
so be yourself!

Be yourself!
Be yourself!
That's all you need!
That's all you need!
So don't go putting on fancy airs
by posing as princes or millionaires
or one day you'll find yourself caught unawares,
so be yourself!

Be yourself!
Be yourself!
That's all you need!
That's all you need!
Life's not intended to be a test,
you don't have to struggle to beat the rest;
God says that you're special, and he should know best,
so be yourself!

God Doesn't Want

Based on Amos 5:21-24
To the tune of *Here we go round the Mulberry Bush*

God doesn't want our fancy prayers,
fancy prayers,
fancy prayers,
God doesn't want our fancy prayers,
if we cannot love our neighbours!

God doesn't want our hymns and songs,
hymns and songs,
hymns and songs,
God doesn't want our hymns and songs,
if we cannot love our neighbours!

God will enjoy our simple prayers,
simple prayers,
simple prayers,
God will enjoy our simple prayers,
when we also love our neighbours.

God will enjoy our hymns and songs,
hymns and songs,
hymns and songs,
God will enjoy our hymns and songs,
when we also love our neighbours.

Dry bones

Dem bones, dem bones, dem dry bones,
dem bones, dem bones, dem dry bones,
dem bones, dem bones, dem dry bones,
I hear de word of de Lord.

Ezekel connected dem dry bones,
Ezekel connected dem dry bones,
Ezekel connected dem dry bones,
I hear de word of de Lord.

Toe bone connected to de foot bone,
foot bone connected to de ankle bone,
ankle bone connected to de leg bone,
leg bone connected to de knee bone,
knee bone connected to de thigh bone,
thigh bone connected to de hip bone,
hip bone connected to de back bone,
back bone connected to de shoulder bone,
shoulder bone connected to de neck bone,
neck bone connected to de head bone,
I hear de word of de Lord.

Dem bones, dem bones, g'on walk a-roun',
dem bones, dem bones g'on walk a-roun',
dem bones, dem bones g'on walk a-roun',
I hear de word of de Lord.